Praise for *18 Minutes with Jesus*

"A life-changing message in just eighteen minutes—what a concept. Dr. Robert Jeffress breaks open the ageless lessons of perhaps Christ's greatest sermon. Dr. Jeffress is not someone who wastes words, and page after page of this book is packed full of powerful thoughts and revelations that will change your life."

Jentezen Franklin, senior pastor of Free Chapel
and *New York Times* bestselling author

"In this new volume from the prolific pen of Robert Jeffress, in his own unique convincing and convicting style, he reveals that this most famous of all sermons is not just an offering of lengthy, lofty platitudes but is most applicable for every aspect of our daily lives. While you may be able to read the Sermon on the Mount in eighteen minutes, it takes a lifetime to incarnate all its truths. Read it. . . and reap!"

O. S. Hawkins, PhD, former pastor of First Baptist Church,
Dallas, and author of the bestselling Code series of devotionals

"In an ever-changing world and culture, Dr, Jeffress unpacks for us the never-changing words of Jesus. If you long to finish well, dive into these powerful truths."

Sheila Walsh, cohost of *Life Today* and author
of *Holding On When You Want to Let Go*

"This an important resource for anyone who is ready to have their perspective shifted and their heart challenged, and to experience the fullness of God's kingdom at work in and through their life here on earth. Your spirit will come to a great understanding of how Jesus intended the Sermon on the Mount to impact your life. This book is not just another teaching but a radical invitation to step into all God has destined you to be."

Debbie Lindell, lead pastor of James River Church
and author of *She Prays*

Praise for *Invincible*

"Are you having difficulty believing you are a conqueror in Jesus Christ? In *Invincible* you will be encouraged to face the big mountains in your life and learn to live a life of boldness for God. You will benefit significantly from Dr. Jeffress's biblical insights on how to overcome doubt, guilt, anxiety, discouragement, fear, bitterness, materialism, loneliness, lust, and grief that are ravishing your life."

Jason Jimenez, founder of Stand Strong Ministries and
bestselling author of *Challenging Conversations*

"There is often pressure in church to act as if you have it all together. 'Don't bring your doubt, anxiety, fear, or guilt in this place!' *Invincible* pushes back against this kind of phony faith and gives us the freedom to acknowledge our struggles. With humor, compassion, and practical advice, Dr. Jeffress provides a way to overcome the mountains we all face and encourage one another on our faith journey. This book is for real people who want real change."

Michael C. Sherrard, pastor and author of *Why You Matter*

Praise for *Courageous*

"With all the uncertainty in our world right now, this new book by my friend Robert Jeffress is a welcome encouragement for believers. His Bible-based tips on thriving during challenging times are not only practical and easy to understand but will help you to stand strong in your faith and live victoriously."

Robert Morris, founding and lead senior pastor of Gateway
Church and bestselling author of *The Blessed Life*,
Frequency, and *Beyond Blessed*

"When it comes to living out biblical principles, we quickly discover we're in an unfriendly culture. Ephesians 5:11 tells us to 'Have nothing to do with the fruitless deeds of darkness,' so how then do we build bridges to skeptics and cynics? How do we win wicked people with antagonistic agendas to the side of our Savior? In his remarkable new book, *Courageous*, Dr. Jeffress shows us page-by-page how to live as winsome and effective ambassadors for Jesus Christ, all so that the perishing will come to salvation and God will receive the glory! I give this book a double thumbs-up!"

Joni Eareckson Tada, Joni and Friends
International Disability Center

WHAT
EVERY
CHRISTIAN
SHOULD
KNOW

WHAT EVERY CHRISTIAN SHOULD KNOW

10 CORE BELIEFS

FOR STANDING STRONG IN A SHIFTING WORLD

DR. ROBERT JEFFRESS

BakerBooks

a division of Baker Publishing Group
Grand Rapids, Michigan

Published by Baker Books
a division of Baker Publishing Group
PO Box 6287, Grand Rapids, MI 49516-6287
www.bakerbooks.com

Printed in the United States of America

Library of Congress Cataloging-in-Publication Data
Names: Jeffress, Robert, 1955– author.
Title: What every Christian should know : 10 core beliefs for standing strong in a
    shifting world / Dr. Robert Jeffress.
Description: Grand Rapids, MI : Baker Books, a division of Baker Publishing
    Group, [2023] | Includes bibliographical references.
Identifiers: LCCN 2022018479 | ISBN 9781540902122 (cloth) | ISBN 9781493439553
    (ebook)
Subjects: LCSH: Theology, Doctrinal—Popular works.
Classification: LCC BT77 .J3475 2023 | DDC 230—dc23/eng/20220706
LC record available at https://lccn.loc.gov/2022018479cip info]

Published in association with Yates & Yates, www.yates2.com.

Baker Publishing Group publications use paper produced from sustainable forestry practices and post-consumer waste whenever possible.

23   24   25   26   27   28   29   7   6   5   4   3   2   1

To the wonderful members
of First Baptist Church of Dallas

Thank you for standing firm
on the sure foundation
of God's Word for 155 years.
"The grass withers, the flower fades,
but the word of our God stands forever"
(Isa. 40:8).

CONTENTS

ACKNOWLEDGMENTS

Our Christian faith rests on pillars that stand strong and immovable, even in our shifting world. I'm grateful not only for these pillars of faith but also for the "pillars" God has put in my own life—the men and women who consistently support, encourage, and strengthen me. I'm especially thankful for the talented team God provided for this book, including:

Brian Vos, Mark Rice, Lindsey Spoolstra, and the whole team at Baker Books, the best publishing partner I've ever worked with.

Randy Southern and Jennifer Stair, who were instrumental in crafting and polishing the message of this book.

Sealy Yates, my literary agent and longtime friend, who provides wise counsel and encouragement.

Carrilyn Baker, my extraordinary executive associate, who expertly oversees the work of our office with a joyful attitude, and Mary Shafer, who assists Carri-lyn and me in innumerable ways.

Ben Lovvorn, executive pastor of First Baptist Dallas, and Nate Curtis, Patrick Heatherington, Ben Bugg, and the Pathway to Victory team, who extend the message of this book to millions of people around the world.

I'm deeply grateful for the support I receive from my wonderful daughters, Julia and Dorothy; my son-in-law, Ryan Sadler; and my beloved triplet grandchildren, Barrett, Blake, and Blair.

And at the very top of the list of people for whom I am most grateful is my wife, Amy. Thank you for your strong support and unconditional love.

INTRODUCTION

Why Theology Matters

Theology isn't what you'd call an attention-grabbing word. If you're like most people, you probably don't lean in when you hear somebody mention it in conversation. And if you do respond to the word *theology*, you might do so in one of several ways.

Perhaps, like a lot of Christians, you respond with indifference. You treat theology the way you treat legal advice, plumbing issues, and auto repair: as something best left to professionals. If an emergency arises and you need a quick answer to a question about premillennialism, you figure you can talk to your pastor.

Maybe you react with annoyance. Theology seems like a needless complication of what should be a simple faith.

Perhaps you react with zealous intensity. You treat each tenet of Christian theology as a purity test, a way of determining who's with you and who's against you.

Or maybe you react with a sense of embarrassment. You

avoid talking about theology because you're afraid your faith will be exposed as shallow.

All of these, and more, are understandable and relatable reactions to the subject of theology. And this book aims to change every one of them.

In the pages that follow, you'll learn ten core beliefs of Christianity. We can think of these ten principles as pillars, the support structures on which our faith is built. But these are no ordinary pillars. They stand strong and immovable, even when the ground under us starts to give way.

The House of Christianity

Let me illustrate what I mean by the pillars of Christianity. Imagine for a moment that Christianity is a massive house with many rooms and architectural features. Now picture in your mind's eye that this house, like the Lincoln Memorial and other famous structures, is surrounded by magnificent, stately columns—or pillars.

In our imaginary house of Christianity, these ten pillars represent the core tenets of Christian theology. Together, they form the supports on which the entire house rests. Without these pillars, the house would collapse.

Within the boundaries of this house, God provides everything we need for spiritual nourishment and growth. We can find the fruit of the Spirit and a deeper understanding of God's Word there.

Within the boundaries of this house, God offers shelter and protection. When difficulties arise, tragedy strikes, or doubts occur, we can take refuge and find comfort, healing, and reassurance.

Within the boundaries of this house, God surrounds us with allies. These people worship with us, affirm us, and challenge us. They provide for us and look to us to provide for them.

In this house, there are countless ways to enjoy life with God and others. But if we venture beyond the structure supported by the ten pillars, we are no longer in the house. That's why it's essential to recognize them.

The borders of Christian theology aren't intended to restrict us or keep others out. They're meant to outline the area in which we can thrive in our understanding of God's Word, grow in our relationship with Jesus Christ, and fulfill the purposes for which we were created.

Practically Speaking

Why does theology matter? And what real difference does it make in our lives today?

We have to correct the mistaken idea that theology is helpful only in doctoral dissertations or debates in seminary coffee shops. The core beliefs of Christianity affect every part of our lives. These foundational principles have practical applications in our families, our friendships, our careers, our priorities, and our self-images. They shape the way we understand and interact with the world around us.

Here's a preview of some of the practical issues we'll address in the chapters that follow.

God's Word

Does the Bible really claim to be God's Word? How can it be God's Word if it was written by human beings? Can we trust the Bible's claims and promises? This chapter will unlock truths about the Bible that will guide you in studying and growing from God's Word.

God the Father

How has God revealed Himself to us? What does it mean that He is holy, all-powerful, and immanent? How can we communicate with Him? This chapter will explore the character of God the Father and help you strengthen your relationship with Him.

God the Son

What did Jesus do before He came to earth? How did He reveal the nature of God? Why is it important that He experienced the same kinds of temptation, conflict, and suffering we do? This chapter answers difficult questions about Jesus's life, teachings, sacrifice, and return.

God the Holy Spirit

What does it mean that the Holy Spirit dwells in believers? How can we grow the fruit of the Spirit in our lives? What are some of the spiritual gifts the Holy Spirit has given us? This chapter reveals the extraordinary things the Holy Spirit can do in and through us, if we allow Him to.

Angels and Demons

What are angels, and what role do they play in God's plan? What strategies does Satan use against us? How can we defend ourselves against demonic forces? This chapter shines a light on the spiritual battle raging all around us and provides a battle plan for defeating our invisible enemy.

Humanity and Sin

What was God's original plan for His human creation? Why did God give us free will? How does sin affect our relationship with God? This chapter shows us how to reclaim what God originally intended for us.

Salvation

Why do we need to be saved? Why did God demand a perfect sacrifice for sin? How should we respond to people who say it's intolerant to claim that there is only one way to heaven? This chapter helps us grasp the difficult issue of exclusivity that lies at the heart of God's plan of salvation.

The Church

Why is worship important in our relationship with God? How does fellowship with other Christians affect our spiritual health? What does it mean to be part of the body of Christ? This chapter reveals the vital role the church plays in our lives—and the vital role we play in the church.

Future Things

How should we interpret biblical prophecies about the future? What difference do these prophecies make in our daily walk with Christ? When will God judge evil once and for all? This chapter reveals God's final plan for the world and offers a glimpse of what awaits us in eternity.

Christlikeness

What is God's plan for our lives? What role does the Holy Spirit play in helping us say no to sin? How can we develop the attitudes and characteristics of Christ? This chapter provides practical strategies to become more like Christ and live in freedom and victory.

Exclusively Inclusive

Before we dive into our study of these ten core beliefs, let me address a question you may be asking: "Do we still need these ten foundational teachings of Christianity? I mean, things have changed a lot in the past two thousand years, and people are offended by some Christian beliefs. Can't we just all get along and believe anything we want to believe?"

I understand why the idea of inclusiveness is extremely popular in our culture today. Inclusiveness invites everyone to the party and makes everyone feel equally welcomed. Inclusiveness says, "Whatever you believe is fine, as long as it doesn't offend anyone. If you validate my truth, I'll validate yours, and we can all walk away feeling validated."

At first glance, the core beliefs of Christianity appear to pop the balloons and tear down the streamers of the inclusiveness party. At the core of the tenet of God the Son lie these words of Jesus: "I am the way, and the truth, and the life; no one comes to the Father but through Me" (John 14:6). It's hard to imagine a more exclusive sentence.

Yet bound tightly to that sentence is another statement by Jesus: "For God so loved the world, that He gave His only begotten Son, that whoever believes in Him shall not perish, but have eternal life" (3:16). It's hard to imagine a more inclusive word than "whoever." God desires to include everyone in His family, but He wants us to know there is only one way for that to happen.

You see, the core beliefs of Christianity run much deeper than the ideas of inclusiveness and exclusiveness. They deal with the very notion of truth. They acknowledge the reality that not all so-called truths are equally valid. They elevate God's truth, as presented in His Word. They build a compelling case for the Christian faith. And in a world that is constantly shifting and growing increasingly hostile to Christianity, these ten pillars offer us something solid, something reliable, and something that remains stable throughout shifting cultural trends and social upheavals.

A Final Challenge

So why should you read this book about Christian theology? The exploration of the ten core beliefs in this book isn't prep work for some graduate-level theology exam. It isn't a vocabulary-building exercise to help you impress your Bible study group with words like *omnipotent* and *pretribulation*. Theology isn't academic, and it isn't religious busywork.

This book is for people who . . .

- long for a deeper relationship with God.
- dare to ask, "Why?"
- bristle at Christian clichés.
- struggle to live like Jesus.
- aren't sure how to respond to our culture's shifting ideas of truth.
- desire to help other believers who are struggling with their faith.

1

GOD'S WORD

A few years ago, former FBI agent Joe Koenig published a book called *Getting the Truth: "I Am D. B. Cooper,"* in which he claimed to have uncovered the identity of the notorious skyjacker who captured headlines in 1971 and the imaginations of mystery lovers ever since.

On November 24, 1971, during a flight from Portland to Seattle, a passenger using the alias "Dan Cooper" told a flight attendant he had a bomb. He demanded $200,000 and four parachutes. When the plane landed in Seattle, authorities delivered the money and parachutes. Cooper released the other passengers and ordered the plane to take off again. Somewhere over southwestern Washington, he parachuted out of the plane with the money and was never seen again.

Nine years later, almost $6,000 of the ransom money was discovered along the banks of the Columbia River. And though the FBI investigated for forty-five years, no trace of the man known as D. B. Cooper has been found. Yet his notoriety endures. Today, you can listen to dozens of podcasts dedicated to the case.

Understandably, Joe Koenig's book caused quite a stir. Based on years of investigation, Koenig identified a Detroit-area man named Walter Reca as the real D. B. Cooper.[1]

Koenig's book is an enjoyable read. It presents a compelling case for its claims. Yet it's nothing more than a pleasant diversion for armchair detectives and true-crime junkies—because, ultimately, there's very little at stake in it. Walter Reca died in 2014, so there's no one to punish and no justice to be meted out.

I can't say whether Joe Koenig's conclusion about Walter Reca is reliable or not. But there's not much riding on its trustworthiness. The answer his book provides isn't provable. Nor is it very important—just an interesting piece of trivia, a fascinating tidbit to share at dinner parties.

On the other hand, the book we call the Bible is anything but trivial. It claims to be transformational. And unlike in Koenig's book, the answers the Bible provides are not only important but, for every person in the entire world, they are literally the difference between life and death.

The Bible Tells Me So

A book about the core beliefs of Christianity must begin with God's Word. If we picture these beliefs as ten pillars, then God's Word is the first pillar we must look at, because it is the one that informs us about the other nine.

The nine core beliefs that follow will involve some extraordinary claims—claims far more consequential and profound than anything Joe Koenig ever proposed. And each of these claims invites a simple yet essential question:

> God the Father is omniscient; He knows everything.
> *Says who?*
>
> After His crucifixion, Jesus rose from the dead.
> *Says who?*
>
> Everyone who believes in Jesus will have eternal life.
> *Says who?*

In each case, the answer is God's Word. Or, to put it more musically, "The Bible tells me so."[2] Virtually everything we know about God, Jesus, the Holy Spirit, angels and demons, humanity and sin, salvation, the church, future things, and Christlikeness is found in God's Word. It's the basis of every theological claim of Christianity. It's also the source of personal transformation. Properly understood, the Bible changes our lives.

In architectural terms, God's Word is a load-bearing pillar. If even one area of the Bible is unsound, if there are any cracks in its makeup, the entire structure becomes suspect. So our first order of business is to test the strength and integrity of Scripture. Can we trust God's Word to hold up our Christian beliefs? Is it something we can put our faith in? Is the Bible true?

Why We Can Trust the Bible

If you're like most people, you probably have some questions about the Bible. You may be wondering, "What proof

23

do we have that the events in the Bible actually happened?" Or, "What about all the errors and contradictions in the Bible?"

Answering these questions requires a deep dive into what makes the Bible unique and sets it apart from every other book, including religious texts, such as the Qur'an and the Book of Mormon, that also claim to be the Word of God.

Let's start by looking at three reasons we can trust the Bible.

The Bible Is Inspired

Thomas Edison famously said, "Genius is one percent inspiration and ninety-nine percent perspiration."[3] The apostle Peter famously said the Bible is 100 percent inspiration. Actually, what he said was, "No prophecy [of Scripture] was ever made by an act of human will, but men moved by the Holy Spirit spoke from God" (2 Pet. 1:21).

Peter and the other Bible writers didn't think, *What this world really needs is a Bible, and we're just the people to create it.* Instead, they wrote as they were prompted by God—as they were "moved by the Holy Spirit." The human writers never initiated the writing of Scripture. They were completely dependent on the Lord's inspiration.

Inspiration, in this context, refers to the supernatural process God used to communicate His message through human beings without error. As 2 Timothy 3:16 tells us, "All Scripture is inspired by God and profitable for teaching, for reproof, for correction, for training in righteousness." The Greek word translated as "inspired" literally means "God-breathed," and it illustrates the direct manner in which God worked. God spoke the universe into existence in Genesis 1, and He breathed the Bible into existence in the minds of those who wrote it.

God originated the message in every word of the Bible. He poured that message through the personalities of the writers. He used the emotional outbursts of King David, the angry rebukes of Moses, and the systematic reasoning of Paul to deliver His message. The message was recognizably God's, while the writing styles were recognizably the authors'.

God's guiding hand prevented the original writers from making any mistakes when they penned the words of Scripture. That's how fallible people were able to produce an infallible Bible.

Some passages, such as the Ten Commandments in Exodus 20 and the messages to the seven churches in Revelation 2–3, contain God's direct dictation. God said, "Write these words," and the writers obeyed. Other passages, such as the Genesis account of creation, involve God revealing truths the writers had no way of knowing. However, most of the Bible was composed by the writers under the Holy Spirit's guidance.

The theological belief that every Bible writer was supernaturally inspired and directed by God is bolstered by the second of the Bible's unique features: its unity.

The Bible Is Unified

If you've ever had to do a group project, you know how challenging it can be to get a roomful of people with diverse personalities and experiences to complete a single assignment. Imagine having to do a group project with forty people from all over the world, before the invention of the internet, over the span of fifteen hundred years! How do you think that project would turn out?

The Bible is the most successful group project in history—one that was directed by God Himself. More than forty people wrote the various books of Scripture over a period of fifteen hundred years. Moses, the first named writer, began work on the first five books of the Old Testament around 1440 BC. The apostle John wrote the last book of the Bible around AD 95.

The forty-some people who recorded and composed God's message were a diverse lot. Moses was a political leader. David was a shepherd. Solomon was a king. Luke was a doctor. Paul was a rabbi. Peter was a fisherman. Each writer had his own personality, his own perspective on the world, and his own peculiarities.

This diverse cast of characters composed the Bible in a variety of locations spread out across some two thousand miles, from Babylon to Jerusalem to Rome. Scripture was written in settings that included deserts, cities, and dungeons. The writers didn't even stick to one literary style. They wrote history, law, poetry, allegory, biography, personal correspondence, prophecy, and apocalyptic literature.

With so many moving pieces and so many variables factoring into its creation, there's no earthly reason for the Bible to function as one organic book—a unified whole far greater than the sum of its parts. Yet it does. The ties that bind the Bible's parts together are unmistakable. The themes of sin and redemption, justice and grace, faith and forgiveness begin in Genesis and weave their way through the entire narrative, all the way to the end of Revelation.

The only explanation for such unity in a book that was composed under such varied circumstances is that a divine Author oversaw the final product.

As with inspiration, the unity of the Bible gives us reason to trust its integrity. Yet the fact remains that human beings were involved in creating God's Word. For better or worse, these forty people were a lot like us—well-intentioned but mistake-prone. So how do we explain Christianity's core belief that the Bible is inerrant?

The Bible Is Inerrant

Critics argue that the Bible doesn't claim to be the inerrant Word of God. They suggest that modern-era fundamentalists came up with the concept of inerrancy as a way of promoting conservatism.

The Bible, on the other hand, makes a different claim. Hundreds of Old Testament passages contain a variation of the phrase, "The Lord said," including these:

- "Then *God spoke* all these words" (Exod. 20:1).
- "Listen, O heavens, and hear, O earth; for *the LORD speaks*" (Isa. 1:2).
- "The words of Jeremiah . . . to whom *the word of the LORD came*" (Jer. 1:1–2).

Psalm 95:7 contains the words, "Today, if you would hear His voice." The human writer of these words isn't identified in the psalm. But nearly a thousand years later, the writer of Hebrews in the New Testament identified the author of Psalm 95 as the Holy Spirit: "Therefore, just as *the Holy Spirit says*, 'Today if you hear His voice'" (Heb. 3:7).

Jesus believed in the inspiration and inerrancy of the Old Testament. He affirmed the Genesis account of creation and

God's blueprint for marriage (Matt. 19:4–6). He used the story of Jonah to illustrate His resurrection (12:39–40). He linked His second coming with Noah's building of the ark (24:37–39). Jesus's confidence in the Old Testament extended beyond stories and individual words to include even the letters and strokes that make up each word (5:17–18).

Some New Testament writers referred to their contemporaries' works as "Scripture." For example, in defending his call to pay those who preach, Paul wrote, "The Scripture says, 'You shall not muzzle the ox while he is threshing,' and

WHO ELSE BELIEVED IN THE BIBLE'S INERRANCY?

Belief in the inerrancy of Scripture continued after the New Testament was written.

- Irenaeus, speaking for the ancient Greek church, wrote, "The Scriptures are indeed perfect, since they were spoken by the Word of God and His spirit."[4]
- Augustine, representing the Western church, said, "The canonical writings are free from error."[5]
- Martin Luther, the leader of the Protestant Reformation, declared, "Holy Scriptures cannot err."[6]
- John Wesley, the founder of Methodism, concluded, "If there be one falsehood in that book, it did not come from the God of truth."[7]

The testimony of these church leaders provides compelling evidence that the inerrancy of Scripture was widely believed during early church history.[8]

'The laborer is worthy of his wages'" (1 Tim. 5:18). The first quote is from Deuteronomy 25:4, which was written almost fifteen hundred years earlier. The second quote is from Luke 10:7, which was written only a few years before Paul's letter. Yet both were Scripture, as far as Paul was concerned.

The apostle Peter returned the favor in 2 Peter 3:15–16, where he referred to the letters of Paul as part of "the Scriptures."

I like the way my mentor and seminary professor Dr. Charles Ryrie put it: "The Bible tells the truth."[9] Needless to say, anything that claims to tell "the truth" is going to get strong pushback. After all, there's no way to prove conclusively that the Bible is God's inspired and inerrant Word, just as there's no way to prove conclusively that God exists. Therefore, the evidence we offer in support of the Bible's inerrancy must be compelling.

Evidence for the Trustworthiness of the Bible

The body of evidence supporting Scripture's trustworthiness is large and convincing. Let's take a look at four specific areas.

Evidence #1: The Dates of the New Testament Books

Most of the New Testament was written between AD 40 and 65. Scholars reached that conclusion because none of the books mentions the destruction of the Jerusalem temple—one of the most momentous events in Jewish history—which occurred in AD 70.

The Gospel of Mark, the earliest of the New Testament books, was written only a few years after Jesus's death and resurrection. This timeline is important because it was too soon for myths to have worked their way into the New Testament narrative.

Plenty of witnesses to the ministry of Jesus were still alive when the New Testament writers put pen to papyrus. Jesus's words were still fresh in the minds of His followers. If Matthew, Mark, Luke, John, Paul, James, Peter, Jude, or the writer of Hebrews had said anything that misrepresented Jesus or His message, there were thousands of people who could have called out their lies, exaggerations, or mistakes. Yet there's no evidence in history of any such reaction. Essentially, thousands of would-be critics with firsthand knowledge of these events heard or read the words of the New Testament and said, "Yeah, that sounds right."

Evidence #2: The Earliest Reactions to the Message

One of the strongest arguments for the truthfulness of the Bible—especially the New Testament—is that its message was embraced quickly by the early followers of Christianity. The New Testament writers, the majority of whom were devout Jews, replaced basic tenets of Judaism with new beliefs. They abandoned the sacrificial system that had been in place for fourteen hundred years. They changed their day of worship to the first day of the week. They replaced circumcision as the sign of faith with baptism. They relegated the law of Moses to a shadow of the newer revelation from Jesus Christ (Col. 2:17).

This dramatic shift in beliefs and practices wasn't limited to the New Testament writers. Almost overnight, thousands of Jews radically altered their most cherished religious convictions and embraced a new spiritual paradigm. The "overnight" event that spurred this shift was the resurrection of Jesus Christ.

The actions of Jesus's disciples testify to the truth of their resurrection claims. While religious zealots throughout history have died for false beliefs they thought were true, no rational person would die for a belief he or she knew was a lie.

The disciples were willing to endure imprisonment, torture, and death rather than recant their testimony that they had seen Jesus Christ in His resurrected body. Surely one of those eleven men would have broken under such pressure and revealed the truth if the disciples had conspired to perpetrate a myth. Instead, the disciples maintained their story until the very end. The reality of Christ's resurrection was embraced so quickly by so many people that, in three hundred years, the faith of those eleven men effectively toppled the Roman Empire. Such is the power of a truthful message.

Evidence #3: Fulfilled Prophecies

One of the strongest arguments for the credibility of the Bible is fulfilled prophecies of Scripture. Detailed predictions about specific individuals, nations, and events were foretold hundreds of years before they occurred, and their fulfillments have been historically verified.

For example, in about 700 BC, the prophet Isaiah predicted that Babylon—a relatively minor player on the world scene at the time—would conquer Judah and take its people captive (Isa. 39:5–6). His prediction came true in 586 BC when Babylon prevailed over Judah. Isaiah also predicted that Babylon would be conquered by another nation (21:9).

What's more, the prophet identified *by name* the king who would allow the people of Judah to return from exile

WHAT ARE THE ODDS?

The mathematical probability that one man in history could fulfill all sixty-one biblical prophecies of the Messiah is so astronomical it can't be computed. So one mathematician cut the number to just eight prophecies. He calculated the probability of one man in history fulfilling eight specific prophecies as 1 in 10^{17}. That's a 1 followed by 17 zeros.

Imagine covering the state of Texas in silver dollars two feet deep. On one of those silver dollars, you draw an X. You blindfold a person and let her roam the entire Lone Star State until she reaches down and picks up one silver dollar. The odds that she would choose the one with the X on it is roughly 1 in 10^{17}—the same odds of one man fulfilling just eight Old Testament prophecies of the Messiah.[10]

Jesus's fulfilling all *sixty-one* prophecies cannot be chalked up to coincidence—or anything other than nearly irrefutable evidence of the Bible's truthfulness.

in Babylon to rebuild Jerusalem. Isaiah 44:28 refers to Cyrus as the king of Persia—one hundred years before Cyrus was born! History tells us that Cyrus, king of Persia, conquered Babylon in 539 BC. In 538 BC, King Cyrus decreed that the Israelites could return to their homeland, just as Isaiah had predicted 150 years earlier.

The New Testament reveals even more amazing examples of fulfilled prophecies, all centered on Jesus Christ. There are at least sixty-one prophecies in the Old Testament concerning the Messiah that were fulfilled by Jesus Christ. These prophecies, made hundreds of years before the fact, include the place of Jesus's birth (Mic. 5:2), the time of His birth (Dan. 9:25), the manner of His birth (Isa. 7:14), the manner of His death (Ps. 22:16), and His burial in a rich man's tomb (Isa. 53:9).

Evidence #4: Archaeological Discoveries

There was a time when archaeology was seen as a real-world audit of the Bible's claims. Critics asked, "If the Bible is true, then why is there no evidence in the historical record of David or Solomon, Israel's two greatest kings? Or the cities of Sodom and Gomorrah? Or the walls of Jericho?"

They pointed to names that appeared only in Scripture and nowhere else in archaeology—names like Ashpenaz, from the book of Daniel; the Hittites, an Old Testament tribe; and Pontius Pilate, the governor who turned Jesus over for crucifixion—as reasons to question the Bible's veracity.

But a funny thing happened on the way to declaring the Bible historically unreliable. Several funny things, in fact. An inscription dating from the ninth century BC was discovered. This inscription referred to the house of David and to the king of Israel. An excavation in Megiddo, one of Solomon's five chariot cities according to the Old Testament, uncovered thousands of chariot stalls.

Clay tablets dating back to 2500 BC were discovered in northern Syria. These tablets mentioned the cities of Sodom and Gomorrah, as well as major earthquake activity in the region. An excavation of the city of Jericho revealed evidence of a sudden collapse of the walls that protected the city.

A brick containing the name Ashpenaz was found in the ruins of ancient Babylon. Tablets describing the ancient

Hittites were found by a German professor. An inscription found on a stone slab in Caesarea named Pontius Pilate as a Roman governor.

The list of other archaeological confirmations of biblical names, events, and locations could fill the rest of this book. And while such discoveries cannot prove the Bible is true, it's important to note there has never been any discovery that has *disproved* any name, event, or location in the Bible.

Can We Trust the Bible We Have Today?

Even if we concede that God inspired the Bible writers and made sure their words were inerrant, we still can't say for sure that the Bible we have today is trustworthy. Technically speaking, the inspiration and inerrancy apply only to the original manuscripts. The problem is, those original manuscripts vanished long ago into the mists of history.

The Bible we have today is a copy of a copy of a copy . . . and so on. Scribes and scholars throughout history translated the original manuscripts into various languages and laboriously reprinted them by hand, word for word. When the original manuscripts were lost, other scribes and scholars reprinted the copies. And so on.

But did these copies maintain the inspiration and inerrancy of the originals? Can we be sure the copyists didn't make mistakes? How do we know that the Bible we have today is reliable?

Are the Copies of the Bible Accurate?

In answering these questions, we need to consider the number of ancient manuscripts, of both the Old and New

Testaments, that are available to us. Most ancient literary works have very few manuscripts to support their authenticity. There are only seven manuscripts for Plato, ten for Caesar's *Gallic Wars*, and twenty for the historian Tacitus. By comparison, there are over *ten thousand* manuscripts for the Old Testament.

The most significant of these are the Dead Sea Scrolls, which were discovered by a Bedouin herdsman in 1947. The scrolls were sealed in clay jars and hidden in a cave. Written around 100 BC, they include a complete copy of the book of Isaiah and fragments of almost every other book of the Old Testament.

Before the scrolls were discovered, the oldest known copy of the Old Testament was dated around AD 900—nearly one thousand years after the Dead Sea Scrolls were written. The discovery of the Dead Sea Scrolls gave scholars an opportunity to compare copies of the Old Testament that had been created nearly a millennium apart.

Have you ever played the telephone game? A handful of people stand in a line. The first person whispers a message to the second person, who then whispers it to the third person, and so on to the end of the line. The result is usually surprising—and often funny. A simple message such as "The quick brown fox jumped over the lazy dog" gets twisted into something unrecognizable ("He quickly thought of ladies").

In a sense, the discovery of the Dead Sea Scrolls set the stage for the end of a thousand-year-long written version of the telephone game. Scholars would get to see how the words of Isaiah had changed—perhaps even unrecognizably—over a millennium. The circumstances were ripe to expose the unreliability of Bible copyists.

Instead, the scrolls testified to the painstaking accuracy of the copyists. Scholars discovered that 95 percent of the words in the text written in AD 900 matched their counterparts written in 100 BC. The text of Isaiah 53 offers a telling look at the phenomenal accuracy of the Bible copies. Of the 166 words that comprise Isaiah 53, scholars found only seventeen *letters* in question. Ten of those were simply spelling differences. Four letters were related to minor issues like conjunctions. The three remaining letters in question spelled the word *light*, which is found in verse 11. This one questionable word does not alter in any significant way the meaning of the text. After one thousand years of copying 166 words, only one word was in question—and that word was insignificant to the meaning of the text.

The manuscript support for the New Testament is even more overwhelming. Without a doubt, the books of the New Testament were the most frequently copied of any books of antiquity. Today, we have nearly twenty-five thousand copies of portions of the New Testament. Contrast that to Homer's *Iliad*, which is next in terms of the number of available manuscripts, with 643 copies. There is more—and earlier—manuscript support for Jesus Christ in the Gospels than for any other figure in the ancient world, including Julius Caesar and Alexander the Great.

The amount of time between the original books of the New Testament and the earliest existing copies is only several hundred years. Although that sounds like a long time, it isn't when compared to other works of literature. The oldest manuscripts of most classical Greek authors are dated more than one thousand years after the author's death.

Most importantly, these manuscripts reveal how accurately the New Testament was transmitted throughout the centuries. The Greek New Testament contains about twenty thousand lines of text. Only about forty lines are in question because of variations among the manuscripts. That amounts to one page in the two-hundred-page Greek New Testament.

Are the Right Books in the Bible?

God didn't announce that He was creating an Old Testament and then recruit authors to write books one through thirty-nine. He didn't negotiate a five-book deal with Moses. He didn't tell Nehemiah, "I'm going to slot you between Ezra and Esther." He didn't reject the first drafts of Obadiah and Nahum for being too long and say, "I already have enough major prophets! What I need are some *minor* prophets!"

Likewise, the Gospel writers of the New Testament weren't angling to get their biographies attached to the Old Testament. Paul, Peter, and John never stopped in the middle of writing a sentence to ask, "How can I put this more *biblically?*"

In other words, the Bible writers didn't know they were writing the Bible. In fact, the Bible as we know it—the canon of thirty-nine books in the Old Testament and twenty-seven books in the New Testament—didn't exist until long after the Bible writers were dead. The uniqueness of God's Word extends to the way it was compiled.

Most of the Old Testament books were recognized as God's Word as soon as they were written. The books of Moses (Genesis to Deuteronomy) immediately were placed next to the ark of the covenant to remind the Israelites of their importance (Deut. 31:24–26). The book of Joshua

(Josh. 24:26), the books of Samuel (1 Sam. 10:25), and the books of the Prophets (Zech. 7:12) were similarly recognized.

The first Greek translation of the Old Testament, known as the Septuagint, was written between 250 and 150 BC. It contains every book in the Old Testament, which means the Old Testament canon was complete by at the latest 150 BC, and perhaps as early as 400 BC. Jesus affirmed the completeness of the Old Testament by His reverence for the Word of God.

There are equally compelling reasons to believe that the twenty-seven books of our New Testament are the only ones that met the lofty standards for inclusion. Virtually every one of them was written by an apostle (Matthew, John, Paul, Peter) or under the supervision of an apostle (Mark's Gospel was likely supervised by Peter).

The Synod of Hippo, a council of leading Christian bishops, officially ratified the twenty-seven books of the New Testament in AD 393. However, most of those books had been recognized by the early church hundreds of years earlier. Significantly, there has been no attempt to add to or delete from the canon of the New Testament since its ratification at the end of the fourth century.

Couldn't Other Books Be Added to Scripture?

The New Testament writer Jude described the Christian faith as having been "once for all handed down to the saints" (v. 3). The Greek word translated as "handed down" describes an activity that is completed. God has finished depositing all the truth we need to know about Him in the Bible. He is not speaking fresh words to writers today.

That's not to say that the only way God gives us direction is through the Bible. God can lead believers today through prayer, circumstances, wise counsel, and even our desires. Yet we should realize that any revelation from God that people claim to receive apart from the Bible is subjective and therefore subject to error.

Later versions of the Septuagint, the Greek translation of the Old Testament, included additional books, some of which are known as the Apocrypha (which means "hidden" or "doubtful"). However, these books are not part of the Old Testament canon. They don't measure up to the standards required for a book to be recognized as God's Word. For one thing, they were written long after the other books of the Old Testament. For another, they contain historical errors. And none of these books claims to contain the Word of God.

The gnostic gospels, made famous in the Dan Brown book (and the Tom Hanks movie) *The Da Vinci Code*, are excluded from the New Testament. They weren't written by apostles, even though some bear the names of apostles. They were composed between one hundred and two hundred years after the time of Christ, making them far less reliable than the four Gospels, which were written within decades of Jesus's life on earth. Finally, the gnostic gospels were rejected by church leaders because they claimed Jesus was purely a divine spirit, not human.

What the Bible Means for Us Today

Acknowledging that the Bible is inspired, unified, inerrant, canonized, and complete doesn't begin to do justice to its potential. If that's all the Bible is, then it's nothing more than a valuable historical document, a keystone for modern archaeology, a literary marvel, and maybe—just maybe—the

CONTRADICTION? NOT NECESSARILY

Critics argue that contradictions in the Bible make it less than reliable. But does the Bible really contain contradictions? A closer look at a few so-called contradictions tells a different story:

- In 1 Corinthians 10:8, Paul described a plague in the Old Testament that killed 23,000 Israelites. Yet the account by Moses in Numbers 25:9 says 24,000 died. Contradiction? Not necessarily. Paul said 23,000 Israelites "fell in one day," while Moses said the total number of victims was 24,000. Perhaps not everyone who contracted the plague died within twenty-four hours.
- In his account of Jesus's resurrection, Matthew said there was an angel at the tomb. In John's account, there were two angels. Contradiction? Not necessarily. Perhaps Matthew decided to focus on the one angel who spoke, while John was more interested in the total number of angels Mary witnessed when she arrived at the empty tomb.
- Matthew 5-7 and Luke 6 record two versions of Jesus's Sermon on the Mount. Contradiction? Not necessarily. It could be that Jesus preached the same message in two locations at two different times. But a more probable explanation is that some Gospel accounts offer accurate paraphrases of what Jesus said rather than direct quotes. So both accounts capture the essence of Jesus's message.

best evidence we have of an intelligence higher than our own. It's something for museums, history buffs, and aficionados of the supernatural.

But the Bible is more than that. The writer of Hebrews gave us a sense of how much more: "For the word of God is living and active and sharper than any two-edged sword, and piercing as far as the division of soul and spirit, of both joints and marrow, and able to judge the thoughts and intentions of the heart" (4:12).

The Bible Heals

The image of a double-edged blade can be misleading. Certainly, there is an element of weaponry to the Bible. For example, Jesus used Scripture to counter Satan's temptations in the wilderness (Matt. 4:1–11). But a two-edged sword can also be used to free us from the entanglements of wrong thinking and wrong behavior.

- If we believe disobeying God will lead to freedom, we get bound up in misery.
- If we believe we're responsible for our own well-being, we get bound up in worry.
- If we believe money is the key to happiness, we get bound up in greed.
- If we believe revenge is the best response to mistreatment, we get bound up in bitterness.

The Word of God slices through our wrong beliefs, freeing us from the resulting wrong behavior—and saving us from a world of hurt.

41

The blade of God's Word can pierce to the very heart of who we are. That's not an easy job, given our limitless potential for self-delusion. As the prophet Jeremiah said, our hearts are deceitful and cannot be trusted (Jer. 17:9). Only the Bible can reveal our true motives for, say, teaching a Bible-study class, fixing a meal for a bereaved family, or writing a check for a church project.

God's purpose in slicing us open is not to hurt us but to heal us. He is the surgeon who cuts open His patients to remove the tumors of sin destroying their lives. The Great Physician uses the scalpel of His Word to expose sin and bring healing.

The Bible Guides

In Psalm 32:8, God promised, "I will instruct you and teach you in the way which you should go; I will counsel you with My eye upon you." The primary means He uses to guide us is His Word.

David said, "Your word is a lamp to my feet and a light to my path" (Ps. 119:105). The illumination he was talking about is similar to that of a flashlight, something that allows us to see a few feet—not a few miles—ahead of us. God rarely provides us with enough light to see every step we need to take in the future, perhaps so we're not tempted to run ahead of Him. But He promises to give us enough direction to take the *next* step.

The Bible Inspires

The Bible connects us with a wisdom deeper than our own and a power greater than our own. It allows us to see past the mundane aspects of our existence and glimpse the things of God—truths of lasting value, truths that bring joy and fulfillment, truths that change lives.

The Bible tantalizes us with stories of people very much like us—ordinary folks who dared to do something big, who allowed their faith to overrule their fear, and who were used by God to accomplish extraordinary things. Then the Bible encourages us to believe that God can do the same in us. It whispers to our souls, *If not you, then who? If not now, then when?*

A Personal Testimony about God's Word

The core belief of God's Word is not just a theological truth for me; I have experienced the transforming power of Scripture in my own life. When I was in college, several of my liberal professors attacked the Bible and attempted to discredit it. Listening to that steady stream of teaching had a profound effect on me. I stopped reading the Bible and seriously questioned whether I wanted to give my life to preaching it.

However, the exposure to that kind of teaching led me to dive into my own study of Scripture. I wanted to find out for myself if the Bible was true. As a result of my study, I came away with two assurances. First, I gained the assurance of the trustworthiness of the Scripture. I discovered the truth of Isaiah 40:8: "The grass withers, the flower fades, but the word of our God stands forever." I hope you, too, come away from this chapter with the absolute assurance that you can trust the Bible to be God's Word.

Second, I discovered that the Bible has the power to transform my life. God's Word will lift you up above your present circumstances, whatever they are, and give you the confidence that God is working out His plan in not just the world in general but your world in particular. Even when things seem to be out of control, Scripture assures us that God has a plan He is working out. God said in Jeremiah 1:12, "I am watching over My word to perform it."

The Bible—the inspired, inerrant, active Word of God—is the primary tool the Holy Spirit uses to produce change in us. The wisest thing we can do is to commit to studying it, seeking out its treasures, and applying its wisdom to our lives.

2

GOD THE FATHER

Several years ago, two young men walked out of a suburban Chicago church, engaged in a spirited conversation about their beloved Chicago Bears. The NFL draft had just taken place, and their doom-laden words left no doubt as to their feelings about the Bears' top selection.

"What a waste of a first-round pick," one of the men said. "There are so many better players available."

"It's a decision that will set the team back five years, at least," his friend agreed. "We can kiss the playoffs goodbye."

On and on they went as they shuffled along with the Sunday morning crowd heading down the front steps to the parking lot.

"They should just tank this season and try to get a high draft pick next year," one concluded.

"Yeah, I think it's time to tear this team apart and start over," his friend concurred.

Their woeful commiseration was interrupted by a man standing directly behind them who placed a hand on each of their shoulders. They turned around to find themselves face-to-face with Mike Singletary, the superstar defensive captain of the Chicago Bears. The man known as "Samurai Mike," famous for his wild-eyed, fearsome stare.

He leveled that stare at the two young men for just a moment, then he grinned, squeezed their shoulders, and walked away, leaving the two awestruck fans with an encounter they would never forget.

Mike Singletary didn't have to reveal his presence that day. He could have stayed silent when he heard the men discussing his new teammate and not troubled himself. No one would have been the wiser. But in making himself known to these young men, Samurai Mike revealed a little of his character. He showed himself to be understanding, playful, and engaging. In his wake, he left two fans for life. They were humbled but excited that he cared enough to interact with them.

If that seems like an odd introduction to the second core belief of Christianity, God the Father, then consider this: the first chapter of the Bible describes God's creation of the world. The remaining 1,188 chapters, to some degree, describe God's revealing Himself to His creation.

It didn't have to be that way. God the Creator had no responsibility to make Himself known to us. He could have put His creation on display as a world-size art exhibit. He could have used the universe as His own private gallery, visiting it whenever He felt like admiring His work.

He could have treated His creation as an enormous science experiment, making note of what happened when He changed certain variables. He might have viewed His creation as dispassionately as a researcher viewing slides and test tubes. Or He could have treated His creation as the world's most lifelike simulation game, playing when He felt like it and letting it go when He didn't.

Instead, God chose to reveal Himself to His creation. He announced His presence over and over again, to the wonder and astonishment of every created being who has ever encountered Him. Not only did God choose to make Himself known, but He also made Himself available to us. He revealed aspects of His nature. He shared secrets of our inner workings that only our Creator would know. He concerned Himself with our well-being. He laid the groundwork for us to have a relationship with Him forever.

As we examine this second core belief of Christianity, we're going to focus on three aspects of God the Father's generous gesture of making Himself known:

the *how*, the means He uses to reveal Himself,

the *what*, the truths about Himself He chooses to reveal, and

the *what now*, the implications of God's revelation for us.

The How

Let's say you had to make yourself known to someone who knew nothing about you. How would you do it? Would you prepare a detailed résumé listing your background, experience, and accomplishments? Would you create a dating profile sharing your likes, dislikes, and what it takes to have chemistry with you? Would you put together a photo album filled with snapshots of the people, places, and events that shaped you?

God operates on a much grander scale, which is understandable given the limitlessness of what He has to reveal. He makes Himself known to us in ways ranging from the universal to the very personal. We find clues to God's nature in His creative handiwork, His Word, His Son, and His inner working in our lives. Let's start with the universal.

God Reveals Himself through Nature

If you're the parent of a school-age child, chances are your refrigerator door serves as a de facto art gallery filled with finger paintings, art-class homework, pages torn from coloring books, and random doodles. Each little masterpiece is display-worthy because it reflects something about the person who created it. And why not? We are created in the image of God, whose own creative work reveals aspects of Himself.

In the Bible, the psalmist-shepherd-king David saw something of God's nature in the vastness and complexity of the universe He created. In Psalm 8:3–4, David marveled that the one possessing the macro-level skills of designing and sustaining the cosmos also possessed the micro-level skills of caring for human beings.

Likewise, the interconnectedness of the natural world gives us a glimpse of God's perfect planning and design. When Job, the long-suffering Old Testament patriarch, challenged his friends' misunderstanding of the way God works, he offered this advice: "Now ask the beasts, and let them teach you; and the birds of the heavens, and let them tell you. Or speak to the earth, and let it teach you; and let the fish of the sea declare to you. Who among all these does not know that the hand of the LORD has done this, in whose hand is the life of every living thing, and the breath of all mankind?" (Job 12:7–10).

The fact that God provides for even the smallest living things reveals His loving concern. Jesus said, "Consider the lilies" (Luke 12:27), so let's consider them. Lilies bloom season after season, nourished by the nutrient-rich soil of God's design. These nutrients are transported by water that falls from the sky and then eventually released back into the atmosphere as part of a cycle God designed. The lilies absorb energy from sunlight in a God-designed process called photosynthesis. Inside each lily's base is nectar, which attracts bees. As the bees collect this nectar, they transfer pollen from the lily's stamen to other lilies, triggering the reproductive process. Care to guess who designed the pollination process?

Jesus's point was this: if God lavishes such care, such loving concern, and such genius design to ensure that lilies can grow and thrive, then imagine what He does for us—the crown of His creation!

The apostle Paul said of God, "Since the creation of the world His invisible attributes, His eternal power and divine nature, have been clearly seen, being understood through what has been made, so that they are without excuse" (Rom. 1:20). However, despite the overwhelming evidence, and despite the fact that we have no excuse for doing so, we still find ways to misunderstand God and draw faulty conclusions from His creation. So He also reveals Himself in a more direct way.

God Reveals Himself through His Word

As we discovered in our study of the core belief of God's Word, "All Scripture is inspired by God" (2 Tim. 3:16). God the Father delivered His message to a select group of writers He chose Himself. He allowed each writer to use his unique voice to communicate that message while He superintended each writer's work to make sure none of His message got lost in translation. God's message begins with the first word in Genesis and ends with the last word in Revelation. God personally ensured that everything He wants us to know about Himself could be found in His Word.

Are you curious about what pleases and displeases God? I encourage you to read some of His commands and instructions. Here are just a few to get you started:

- "You shall have no other gods before Me" (Exod. 20:3).
- "Honor your father and your mother" (Exod. 20:12).
- "You shall love your neighbor as yourself" (Mark 12:31).
- "Love your enemies" (Matt. 5:44).
- "Flee from youthful lusts" (2 Tim. 2:22).
- "Do all to the glory of God" (1 Cor. 10:31).

These commands, and hundreds of other instructions woven throughout the Bible, do more than reveal aspects of God's nature. Because you and I were created to honor God, His commands also serve as a blueprint for how we can find ultimate fulfillment in life.

In those same pages of Scripture, God underscores His absolute authority. He shows His power over human governments by appointing and removing kings, toppling kingdoms, and defeating armies. He shows His power over nature by parting the Red Sea, turning a rock into a water fountain, and protecting Daniel in a den of starving lions. He shows us His power over death through the miracle of bringing people back to life, which occurs no fewer than ten times in the Bible.

And so on.

One of the most rewarding aspects of God's Word is that every time we read it, we can find a different nuance of God's character—something we hadn't noticed before, something that deepens our awe, appreciation, and love for Him. We see His preference for underdogs in His selection of people like Esther and Gideon to accomplish His will. We see His patience in His dealings with Abraham and Jonah. We see His tender mercy in answering the anguished prayers of Isaac and Hannah.

And at the center of the Bible's narrative, we find the account of an even more personal and sacrificial step that God the Father took to reveal Himself to us.

God Reveals Himself through Jesus

The seeds of this revelation were sown in the garden of Eden when Adam and Eve disobeyed God and ate from the tree of the knowledge of good and evil. Their sin opened a chasm between humans and God—a divide that could be bridged only by a perfect sacrifice, which could be made only by the Son of God. So God sent His only Son, in human form, to earth, where He lived a sinless life, suffered and died for our sins, and then conquered death through His resurrection. Because of Jesus's sacrifice, anyone who believes in Him will have eternal life.

Amazingly, one of the things that gets overlooked in this story of the most profound act of love ever recorded is that, for thirty-three years, God Himself dwelled among us. He walked with us, ate with us, and laughed with us. He knew what it was like to be loved and hated. He subjected Himself to the same temptations we face, the same annoyances we endure, the same rejection we experience, and the same pain we feel.

Around age thirty, Jesus—God the Son—began His public ministry. He made Himself known, first to a small group of followers and then to an ever-widening circle. For the next three years, those who believed in Him and recognized Him for who He was had front-row seats to deity in action. A few of them would later commit their eyewitness accounts to papyrus for the whole world to share.

For a sizable group of people, the question "What is God like?" was no longer an abstract theological musing. They could literally point to Him. "See that plain-looking guy over there? The lowly carpenter's son from Nazareth? The one touching that leper? The one who hangs out with tax collectors, prostitutes, and the other dregs of society? The one who said we should love our enemies? The one the Jewish religious leaders said was demon-possessed? Well, say hello to God."

Because Jesus was fully human and fully God, He revealed God the Father in everything He said and did. In John 14:9, Jesus said so Himself: "He who has seen Me has seen the Father." (We'll see much more of how God the Father reveals Himself through Jesus when we examine the core belief of God the Son.)

God Reveals Himself through His Spirit

God wasn't content merely to become human. Amazingly, He reveals Himself to us in an even more personal way. Everyone who accepts the gift of salvation that Jesus's sacrifice makes possible also receives a bonus gift: God the Holy Spirit takes up residence in our being. God Himself dwells inside us.

The Holy Spirit makes Himself known through our consciences. When we make decisions that please Him, He triggers in us a sense of connection with Him. When we follow the path He's laid out for us in the Bible, He gives us a sense of fulfillment in our lives. Likewise, when we make decisions that displease Him or pursue a path that leads us astray, He pricks our consciences. Working at a soul-deep level, the Holy Spirit lets us know that things aren't right.

God works through His Spirit to help us grasp things about Himself that are difficult to understand. Paul said God reveals all He has prepared for those who love Him "through the Spirit; for the Spirit searches all things, even the depths of God" (1 Cor. 2:9–10). (We'll see much more of how God reveals Himself through His Spirit when we examine the core belief of God the Holy Spirit.)

The What

The news that God the Father reveals Himself to us is remarkable. But it raises an inevitable question: What is it that God reveals? What exactly does He want us to know about Himself? Let's look at three things we can discover about God by observing nature, reading His Word, studying the life and teachings of Jesus, and listening to the Holy Spirit.

God Reveals His Attributes

God's attributes are the characteristics and traits that help us appreciate God's absolute uniqueness. But where do we begin? Trying to nail down God's attributes is like trying to take a panoramic picture of the ceiling of the Sistine Chapel. There's no way to get everything into focus and give the details the attention they deserve.

With that in mind, let's narrow our focus to ten attributes that give us a good starting point in discovering what God is like and a good jumping-off point for further study.

1. *God is holy.* Everything about God is good and right. Sin can't exist in His presence, just as darkness can't exist in bright sunshine. They are mutually exclusive. Because of God's holiness, anyone tainted by sin can't expect to have a personal relationship with Him.

2. *God is just.* God demands punishment for sin. Because He's perfectly just, there are no exceptions. He never looks the other way or lets certain things slide. He requires that every sin be accounted for and punished.

3. *God is loving.* God's love is perfect—something much deeper than a fluttery, feel-good attachment driven by emotions and circumstances. God's profound love involves instruction, correction, discipline, and allowing us to face the consequences of our actions. Because God loves us, He wants what's best for us. More than that, He will do whatever is necessary to make sure that we recognize and pursue what's best for us.

4. *God is eternal.* Time does not apply to God. He'd already lived forever when humans started keeping track of time, and He will exist forever after time ends. He can see the

GOD'S PERFECTIONS

We use words like *traits* and *characteristics* to refer to God's attributes. But *perfections* is a more accurate term. Human traits and characteristics are limited and often in conflict with one another. For example, one person may be intelligent in certain areas but average at best in others. Another may be friendly at times but vengeful when crossed.

On the other hand, every one of God's attributes is perfect and complete. He's not just loving; His love is perfect and complete. He's not simply just; His justice is perfect and complete. His justice never negates His love, and vice versa. His attributes exist in perfect harmony with one another.

entirety of what we call the past, present, and future because He is above it all. God was not created. He is dependent on no one for His existence. We are alive because God created us. God is alive because He is life. We can rest assured that when He says, "I am with you always" (Matt. 28:20) and "I will never desert you, nor will I ever forsake you" (Heb. 13:5), He has the credentials to back it up.

5. God is omnipotent. God's power over the universe is limitless. In fact, the world exists only because God thought it would be a good idea. One word from Him brought the universe, in all its splendor and complexity, into being. He suspends the laws of nature at will to accomplish His purposes, whether it involves causing a ninety-year-old woman to become pregnant (Gen. 21:1–7), stopping the sun's celestial movement so the Israelites could score a military victory

(Josh. 10:1–15), or allowing three of His servants to walk around unharmed in a burning furnace (Dan. 3).

6. *God is omniscient.* God knows everything: past, present, and future. He sees it all because He exists apart from time. He knows how everything in the universe works. He knows why everything happens. He knows everything about us—every good and bad thing we've ever done, everything we're capable of, and every choice we'll ever face. He knows our true motives and our deepest feelings. He knows what the future holds for us. He knows how we can experience ultimate fulfillment and happiness. He knows how we can maximize the gifts He's given us to serve Him and make a difference in the world.

7. *God is immanent.* The word *immanent* means "remaining within; indwelling."[1] God is always present in His creation. In corporate terms, He's a hands-on manager. God didn't create the world and then walk away, leaving us to fend for ourselves. He doesn't rely on angels to bring Him

CAN AND CAN'T

When we discuss God's power, the question inevitably arises: "Can God do *anything*?" Strictly speaking, the answer is no. God can't do anything contrary to His perfect, holy nature. For example, He can't lie (Titus 1:2), be tempted by evil (James 1:13), or be faithless (2 Tim. 2:13), to name just a few things. These are called natural limitations—things God can't do because they go against His nature. These limitations don't make God any less powerful; they just make Him true to His nature.

monthly progress reports. He sees all and stays ever near to us, in good times and bad.

8. *God is transcendent.* God is not constrained by the universe or anything in it. He is completely distinct from His creation. He is not subject to the physical laws of this world. His being is beyond our ability to understand. We know what we know about God only because He chooses to reveal it. God is involved in the daily workings of this world because He chooses to be. He is not compelled to be part of our lives; He wants to be.

9. *God is sovereign.* God is the ultimate authority in heaven and on earth. He answers to no one. God is not obliged to do anything unless He obliges Himself. He doesn't rely on advisors, focus groups, image handlers, or marketing surveys. He isn't motivated by popularity or party loyalty. He does what He wants, when He wants. And everything God does is right and perfect simply because He does it.

10. *God is unchanging.* Old and New Testament writers agree: God is the same yesterday, today, and forever (Heb. 13:8). "God is not a man, that He should lie, nor a son of man, that He should repent" (Num. 23:19). He does not change like a "shifting shadow" (James 1:17). God doesn't phase out old attributes over time and try out new ones. He doesn't rethink His promises in light of recent developments. We can always count on God to be who He says He is and to do what He says He will do.

God Reveals His Names

Let's do a quick exercise: I'll give you a name, and you think hard about everything that comes to mind when you read that name. Ready?

Ronald Reagan.

Unless you're too young to remember our fortieth president, it's likely that some specific images came to mind. You pictured the man's physical features and mannerisms. You recalled his distinctive voice and speaking style. Perhaps you thought about certain moments from his presidency—the assassination attempt or his challenge to Mikhail Gorbachev to tear down the Berlin Wall. You probably recalled things you liked or disliked about him. Maybe you even replayed some scenes from *Bedtime for Bonzo* in your mind. The point is, the name Ronald Reagan stirred a reaction in you. His name represents his entire being, as your name does with you, my name does with me, and God's name does with Him.

Or, in God's case, His *names*. Scholars suggest there are more than one hundred names for God in Scripture. These are names that are known to us only because He revealed them.

Each name gives us unique insight into God's character. Certain names also encourage us to draw nearer to Him as circumstances present themselves in our lives. For example, if you or a loved one is struggling with health issues, you may find special comfort in praying to *Jehovah Rapha*, the Lord our Healer. Or if you're overwhelmed by the beauty of a sunset or a mountain vista, you might find a satisfying outlet for your emotions by offering praise to *El Elyon*, God Most High.

Let there be no confusion: God never changes. There is no difference between *Jehovah Rapha* and *El Elyon*. He is the one true God, regardless of nomenclature. But there's a familiarity—an intimacy—in being able to call God by His various names that serves us well. Consider the different names people use to refer to us. The name they choose reflects their relationship with us. To some people, I'm Dr. Jeffress. To my friends, I'm Robert. To my daughters, I'm Dad. And to my grandchildren, I'm Paw Paw, my new favorite name.

As with God's attributes, there's no way we can do justice to the complexity of God's names. But we can prime the pump for further study. With that in mind, here's an introduction to a few of the names of God.

Elohim is the first name of God used in the Bible—in Genesis 1:1, to be precise. It is the general name for God, and it means "supreme one" or "mighty one."

Yahweh is the name God used to identify Himself to Moses in the burning bush (Exod. 3:13–15). It means "I AM WHO I AM"—or "I AM." Yahweh is the covenant name that refers to God's special relationship with the nation of Israel.

El Elyon means "God Most High" (Ps. 57:2). This is the universal name for God. This name is used to refer to His role as the God of the entire universe.

El Shaddai, or "God Almighty," is the name God used to make Himself known to Abram in Genesis 17:1.

El Roi is the name Hagar used in Genesis 16 when God found her in the wilderness. It means "the God who sees me."

Adonai is a name for God that means "Lord," derived from the Hebrew word for "sovereign."

Abba is an Aramaic word for "father," used in a familiar but respectful sense, much like our English word "Daddy" (Rom. 8:15).

There are many other names of God throughout Scripture, and each one reveals even more of His character. The more we know about the attributes and names of God, the better equipped we are to respond to a third aspect of His revelation: God's plan.

THE NAMES OF JEHOVAH

Jehovah is a variation of the name Yahweh. The Old Testament includes seven names for God that begin with Jehovah:

- Jehovah Jireh means "the Lord our Provider." This is the name Abraham used when God provided a ram for him to sacrifice in Isaac's place (Gen. 22:14).
- Jehovah Rapha means "the Lord our Healer." He heals not just our bodies but also our souls by forgiving our sins (Exod. 15:26).
- Jehovah Nissi means "the Lord our Banner." Banner, in this context, refers to a rallying site, such as where the Israelites gathered in their victory over the Amalekites (Exod. 17:15).
- Jehovah Shalom means "the Lord our Peace." This is the name Gideon used when he saw the angel of the Lord (Judg. 6:24).
- Jehovah Rohi means "the Lord our Shepherd." In his most famous psalm, David compared God's relationship with His people to a shepherd's relationship with his sheep (Ps. 23:1).
- Jehovah Tsidkenu means "the Lord our Righteousness." This name looked forward to God's providing righteousness through the sacrifice of His Son (Jer. 23:6).
- Jehovah Shammah means "the Lord is Here" This name celebrated the glory of the Lord returning to Jerusalem after a long absence (Ezek. 48:35).

God Reveals His Plan

Scottish poet Robert Burns once destroyed a mouse's nest while plowing a plot of land. To make amends, he wrote a poem titled, appropriately enough, "To a Mouse, On Turning Her Up in Her Nest with the Plough." From a translation of this poem, we get the well-known saying, "The best-laid plans of mice and men often go awry."

But what about the best-laid plans of our sovereign, all-powerful, omniscient heavenly Father? God created the world and the human race according to His perfect plan. He gave us free will so that we could choose to love and obey Him. He placed us in an earthly paradise and surrounded us with everything we would ever need, including unfettered access to Him. God and humanity, enjoying perfect fellowship and harmony forever. That was His plan.

It went awry when we chose to pursue sin instead of Him. We grabbed the reins of our free will and drove straight into a chasm. Remember, God is holy. His holiness demands complete separation from sin. He is also just. His justice demands the punishment for sin: death. The only way to restore our relationship with God—the only way to satisfy His perfect holiness and perfect justice—was with a perfect sacrifice.

Somebody who was completely sinless—somebody who deserved no punishment from God—had to step forward to bear the full brunt of God's holy wrath for every sin ever committed. Somebody had to suffer and die in our place.

So God revealed the continuation of His perfect plan. He sent His only Son, Jesus, to earth, where He lived a sinless life and then gave that life in place of ours. Jesus paid God's penalty for our sin. He made it possible for us to restore our relationship with our heavenly Father and have eternal life.

God revealed His plan in the Old Testament hundreds, even thousands of years before Jesus came to earth. He revealed the unfolding of His plan in the four Gospels. And He revealed the implications of His plan throughout Scripture.

God's plan continues to unfold, and there are roles and responsibilities for everyone who chooses to be part of it. Our first responsibility is to receive the salvation Jesus offers. We do that by acknowledging that Jesus alone can save us. We confess our sins and then repent, or turn away from them. We ask God to forgive us. And then we hand the reins of our lives to Him and give Him control.

After we align ourselves with Jesus, God reveals the roles and responsibilities that will shape the rest of our lives. He instructs us to take the Good News that changed our lives to the people in our sphere of influence who need to hear it so that it can change their lives too. And then He asks us to take that message beyond our sphere of influence.

God instructs us to follow Jesus's example in caring for people who slip through the cracks of society. In doing so, He reveals His heart for strugglers and outcasts, for the impaired and the forgotten, for the morally compromised and the emotionally fragile. God asks us to choose first the people who are used to being chosen last.

These and a lifetime's worth of other marching orders are revealed in God's Word. Also there, in John 10:10, are the words of Jesus that reveal the guiding truth threading its way through every part of God's plan: "I came that they may have life, and have it abundantly."

The What Now

God's revealing of Himself—His attributes, names, and plans—is generous beyond anything we could ever hope for. But He didn't stop there. Along with His revelation He includes an invitation: "O taste and see that the LORD is good; how blessed is the man who takes refuge in Him!" (Ps. 34:8). In essence, He says, "Here's who I am. Come and see for yourself."

The question falls to us: What do we do with what we know about God?

We RSVP

When the holy, just, loving, eternal, all-powerful, all-knowing, immanent, transcendent, sovereign, and unchanging Creator and Sustainer of the universe invites us to get to know Him better, we seize the opportunity. We do so by diving deep into Scripture and searching for more about Him, His nature, and His will. In this chapter, we've only scratched the surface of who God is. The Word of God offers a master class on the subject. We can explore His interactions with people in the Old and New Testaments to learn how to build and strengthen a relationship with Him.

We accept God's invitation to get to know Him better by rethinking our approach to prayer. When Jesus taught His disciples to pray in what we call "the Lord's Prayer," He first emphasized the importance of contemplating God's holiness ("Hallowed be Your name," Matt. 6:9). Before we start listing our requests and pouring out our troubles to the Lord in prayer, we ought to focus our full attention on God and His holiness, offering Him our heartfelt praise and adoration. When we reach a mindset of proper reverence, we can "draw near with confidence to the throne of grace, so that we may receive mercy and find grace to help in time of need" (Heb. 4:16).

We accept God's invitation to know Him better by writing about our experiences with Him in a prayer journal, thereby recording the evidence of Him that we see in the world around us, keeping track of answered prayer, and creating a paper trail of His work in our lives that we can revisit whenever we need to.

I have kept a prayer journal for many years. In a spiral notebook, I divide each page into two columns, labeled "My Requests" and "God's Answers." I record all my requests to God and use them as a guide for my praying. When God answers that request with a yes or no, I record it under "God's Answers." Occasionally, when I am discouraged, I flip through my prayer journal and feel my cloud of discouragement dissipate as I remember God's supernatural intervention in my life. But I am equally encouraged when I read some of the "no" answers to my prayers and see how God had a better plan for my life than I could have ever imagined. My prayer journal has been a great source of comfort as I look back and see God's past faithfulness to me.

We Tap into His Resources

If you were looking for a contractor or a consultant to help you with a major project, what qualities would you look for? What words on a business card or in an online review would catch your eye? *Dependable? Conscientious? Professional? Guaranteed? Inexpensive?*

How about *all-powerful?* Or *all-knowing?* Or *immanent*, for that matter—you'd never have to wonder where your contractor was. God's perfections are our most valuable (super) natural resources. They are available to us 24/7, every single day. And they are limitless. We can draw on them daily, even hourly, if necessary.

How often do you and I face temptation? Sure, certain temptations are easy to resist when our willpower is fully charged, when we can see the danger of giving in, or when we're surrounded by people who can help us resist. But not all temptations are so accommodating. Some fly under our radar. They track toward a weak spot in our defenses and land when we're most vulnerable. And we find ourselves powerless to resist. Fortunately for us, our heavenly Father has power to spare. In fact, He has *all* power. And we can draw on as much of it as we need—through praying, memorizing Scripture passages, and other methods—until the temptation subsides.

How often do we struggle with loneliness? How many of us know all too well the sting of being abandoned by friends, feeling alone in a crowd, or being separated from loved ones? In those moments when everyone else seems so distant, our heavenly Father is always near. And when we tap into His immanence, we can find much-needed light in our dark nights of the soul.

Perhaps you're wrestling with the question, "Where do I go from here?" Maybe your life has been temporarily delayed on account of uncertainty. Perhaps you're standing at a crossroads with no direction arrows, or you're frozen by the fear of making the wrong life choices.

What you and I need at times like this is Someone wiser to guide us. Someone who can see the big picture. Someone who can say with absolute certainty, "I know where this path leads, and you're going to like it." We have that Someone available to us, and He invites us to draw on His wisdom and tap into His omniscience. And because He loves us perfectly, we can trust that He will never lead us astray.

We Put Him on the Throne of Our Lives

As we discovered earlier, God's perfections exist in perfect harmony. That means God's loving generosity, as awesome as it is, never overshadows His sovereignty. So while He may freely share His power, presence, and wisdom with us, He will not accept a just-when-we-need-Him role in our lives.

God is supreme over all creation. He answers to no one. His power and wisdom are limitless. He knows every secret the universe holds and every aspect of our being. Why would we expect Him to defer to us in anything? Why would we want Him to?

The final, and most important, answer to the question, "What do we do with what we know about God?" is this: We submit to His authority. We give God complete control of every area of our lives. We do so with a sense of reverence, gratitude, humility, and joy. Then we buckle up for the adventure!

The Whispers of God's Presence

As we wrap up our examination of God the Father, let's look at one of the most extraordinary—and revealing—encounters with the Almighty in Scripture. The story is found in 1 Kings 19. The Old Testament prophet Elijah was depressed because he thought he was about to be martyred for obeying God. To boost Elijah's spirit, God told him to grab a front-row seat on Mount Horeb because He, God the Father, was going to pass by.

In person.

While Elijah watched, a powerful wind tore across the mountain and shattered the rocks all around him. But God wasn't in the wind.

Then a devastating earthquake shook the mountain to its core. But God wasn't in the earthquake.

Following that, a raging fire consumed everything in its path. But God wasn't in the fire.

In the wake of the fire's roar, after perhaps the most awesome parade of natural phenomena ever witnessed, Elijah heard a gentle whisper. In 1 Kings 19:13, we read, "When Elijah heard it, he wrapped his face in his mantle." Why? Because God was in the whisper.

God's presence is as big, bold, and dramatic as the most powerful forces on earth—and as intensely personal as a whisper. The better you get to know Him, the louder that whisper will become in your life.

3

GOD THE SON

One of the quirks of our culture is that we gauge a person's importance in terms of time. Social media celebrities get their fifteen minutes of fame. The guest of honor at a celebration is called the man or woman of the hour. Cities declare honorary days for local celebrities. Libraries promote Shakespeare Week. The Turner Classic Movies network features a Star of the Month. Every December, *Time* magazine selects its Person of the Year. Every tenth year, it selects its Person of the Decade. Certain presidents are given eras by historians—the Roosevelt Era, for example. A handful of British monarchs do them one better with "ages," such as the Elizabethan Age and the Victorian Age.

But only one person divided history in half. Only one life caused us to recalibrate our measurement of existence on earth. Whether you call the resulting halves of history

BC (Before Christ) and AD (*Anno Domini*, the year of our Lord) or BCE (Before the Common Era) and CE (Common Era), the dividing line is the same: the arrival of Jesus Christ.

In keeping with this time theme, we're going to examine the third core belief of Christianity—God the Son—from the perspective of three eras: before He came to earth, while He lived among us, and since His return to heaven.

Jesus BC

My family has several Christmas traditions: we go to the Christmas Eve service at our church, eat beef stew, and open gifts afterward, and we watch our favorite holiday movie, *Elf*. I know families whose Christmas traditions include baking a birthday cake to celebrate the birth of Jesus.

But Christmas marks only Jesus's birth in human form. Jesus didn't start to exist on December 25—or on any other date. Jesus is fully God. He possesses all God's perfections, including His eternal nature. Not only has Jesus existed forever, but He also played key roles in BC history.

The Word

Let's start at the beginning—specifically, the beginning John referred to in the first verse of his Gospel: "In the beginning was the Word, and the Word was with God, and the Word was God." The beloved disciple managed to pack an eternity's worth of content into seventeen words. Let's unpack it, starting with the word . . . *Word*.

In the Old Testament, the Word (or "word of the LORD") refers to an aspect of God's divine being that has a life of its own. In Genesis 1, the Word of the Lord brought creation into existence. In the stories of Abraham (Gen. 15:4), Elijah (1 Kings 18:1), Jeremiah (Jer. 28:12), and others, the Word of the Lord came to individuals, bearing messages from the Almighty. The Word acts as God's agent in accomplishing God's will.

In New Testament times, the Greek word *logos*, or "word," was used to describe that which holds together the universe and gives it meaning. These are the concepts John drew on in John 1:1.

In the beginning was the Word. The Word was around to see the beginning, which means the Word existed *before* the beginning. The Word is eternal.

The Word was with God. The Word is a distinct person in the Godhead. The Word and God are two individual persons.

The Word was God. The Word is one with God. The Word and God are individual persons in one being.

John continued to tell us about the Word through chapter 1 of his Gospel. The Word brought creation into existence (v. 3), revealed God's truth to the world, bringing light to our darkness (vv. 4–5), took human form and lived among us (v. 14), and is Jesus Christ (v. 17).

The Prophecies

One of Jesus's key BC roles was as the subject of biblical prophecy. Before God sent His Son into the world, He did thousands of years of prep work. He wanted to make sure the world would recognize and appreciate what Jesus was going to do. God set up a system of worship and sacrifice that pointed to the once-and-for-all sacrifice that was coming. He sent messengers to make people aware of their sin and their need to repent and be forgiven.

WHY WAS THE VIRGIN BIRTH NECESSARY?

According to 2 Samuel 7:12, the Messiah would come from the lineage of King David. However, one descendant of David, a man named Jeconiah, turned out to be so evil that God pronounced a curse on him. No descendant of Jeconiah would sit on David's throne and rule with prosperity (Jer. 22:30). You can see the problem that created. How could the Messiah inherit the right to rule from David but escape the curse of Jeconiah? The answer is through a virgin birth. Joseph was a descendant of David and Jeconiah, but he was not Jesus's biological father. So Jesus escaped the curse. But because Joseph was Jesus's legal guardian, he was able to pass on the right to rule to Jesus. In this we see the perfect plan of God at work, even in the genealogy of His Son.

Then God told people how they could recognize His Son when He came. Once upon a time, that kind of information was necessary—before we started carrying the equivalent of an FBI database in our phones. Back in the day, if you were expecting to meet someone you didn't know—on a blind date, for example—you needed specific information to help you recognize the person ("I'll be wearing a green shirt and a white hat").

God did something similar in the Old Testament. He wasn't necessarily interested in people being able to recognize Jesus on sight. Instead, He wanted to lay the groundwork for them to be able to confirm His identity as the long-promised Savior and Messiah.

So God spoke through His prophets. The prophet Isaiah passed along these words: "The LORD Himself will give you a sign: Behold, a virgin will be with child and bear a son, and she will call His name Immanuel" (Isa. 7:14). That was about seven hundred years before the angel Gabriel announced to Mary that she would give birth to a child who would save His people, and Mary asked, "How can this be, since I am a virgin?" (Luke 1:34).

The prophet Micah announced that a ruler of Israel would come from Bethlehem (5:2). That was about seven hundred years before Joseph and a very pregnant Mary traveled from their hometown of Nazareth to the city of Joseph's ancestor to register for a tax, as commanded by the Roman emperor Caesar Augustus. Luke 2:1–7 (along with our favorite Christmas carols) tells us what happened next: while they were in the city of David, also known as Bethlehem, Mary gave birth.

David included prophetic details in his psalms that anticipated the events of Jesus's crucifixion, nearly a thousand years before it happened:

- "They pierced my hands and my feet" (22:16).
- "For my thirst they gave me vinegar to drink" (69:21).
- "They divide my garments among them, and for my clothing they cast lots" (22:18).

The fulfillment of these prophecies and others can be found in the crucifixion narratives of Matthew 27, Mark 15, Luke 23, and John 19.

In our discussion of God's Word, we discovered that Jesus fulfilled more than sixty such prophecies during His lifetime. Each one is a gift from God to us. Here in the twenty-first century, we can't physically interact with Jesus. We must take it on faith that He is who He claims to be. But our faith doesn't have to be blind. We have evidence. God said, *Here's what the Savior will do.* And Jesus did those things.

Before we explore the specifics of what Jesus did, we need to consider what it meant for Jesus to become one of us.

The Incarnation

When we think of Jesus's sacrifice, we tend to think of the cross, and the suffering and death He experienced there. But Jesus's sacrifice actually began the moment He took human form, an event known as the incarnation.

Think about it: Jesus is God the Son. He is the Word of God who brought the universe into existence. He possesses all the perfections of God the Father. His power and knowledge are limitless. Nothing can harm Him.

Yet Jesus obediently and willingly laid aside His rights to come to earth and dwell among us. He left His idyllic existence in heaven for a life of rejection, ridicule, and betrayal on our sin-ravaged planet. He gave up His autonomy and became a helpless baby, dependent on His human mother for care and protection. He submitted Himself to physical restrictions such as hunger, thirst, and exhaustion. He squeezed His infinite presence into a container of flesh the size of the average man.

Imagine how restricting the incarnation must have been for Jesus. Imagine the kind of love that motivated Him to make such a sacrifice.

(Thirty-)Three Years That Changed the World

Jesus lived on earth for about thirty-three years. Thirty of them are almost a complete mystery to us. We know Jesus was circumcised when He was eight days old (Luke 2:21). Some forty days later, Joseph and Mary took Him to Jerusalem for a dedication ceremony, according to Jewish tradition (vv. 22–39). After that, Luke's Gospel account of Jesus's childhood fades to black.

When it fades in again, Jesus is almost a teenager. Luke 2:41–50 tells the story of Joseph and Mary finding the twelve-year-old Jesus in the temple, amazing religious scholars with His understanding of Scripture. Fade to black again.

When the Gospel narrative fades in again this time, Jesus is thirty years old and ready to start His public ministry.

If the Gospels were a photo album of Jesus's life, they would feature only one snapshot of Him between the time He was two months old and the time He was thirty years old. Virtually everything we know about Jesus occurred during the last three years of His life.

In just over a thousand days, Jesus went from being a relatively unknown Nazarene to being the central figure in human history. In roughly thirty-six months, He laid the groundwork for a spiritual movement that continues to thrive two thousand years later. In the time it takes many people to choose a college major, Jesus radically altered the way we view the world and the people in it.

How did He do it? To understand the third core belief of Christianity, we have to look at how three years changed everything.

What Did Jesus Do?

In the last verse of his Gospel, the apostle John expressed the sense of futility that biographers of Jesus faced: "There are also many other things which Jesus did, which if they were written in detail, I suppose that even the world itself would not contain the books that would be written" (21:25).

With that in mind, we're not going to attempt a comprehensive listing of Jesus's acts recorded in the Gospels. Instead, we're going to look at three categories of things He did that reveal key aspects of His nature, His earthly ministry, and His expectations for His followers.

Jesus Defied Expectations

First, during His earthly ministry, Jesus defied expectations. If the Bible shows us anything, it's that there's no gift, command, or teaching from God that humans cannot misuse, misapply, or misunderstand. Our track record is embarrassingly consistent in that regard.

God gave His law to Moses to reveal Himself and to show His people how to live. More than that, though, He wanted them to recognize their need for a Savior. The law not only sets the standard for righteousness but also reveals just how far we fall short of it. In Romans 3:20, Paul said, "Through the Law comes the knowledge of sin."

Unfortunately, Jewish religious leaders turned the law into a rule-obeying contest. They created an elaborate system of extra laws designed to keep people from even coming close to breaking one of God's actual laws. For example, God said, "Remember the sabbath day, to keep it holy" (Exod. 20:8).

The religious leaders, in turn, created a list of things people could and couldn't do on the Sabbath. They went so far as to decide how many steps people could take and what they were allowed to lift on that day. Naturally, these keepers of the law expected that the Messiah would be a master rule-follower Himself, someone whose every word and action met their strict criteria.

Likewise, as we discovered earlier, God delivered prophecies so that His people would recognize the Savior when He came. Unfortunately, many Jewish people chose to interpret these prophecies in ways that fit their own agendas.

Jesus arrived at a desperate time in Israel's history. The nation was under the thumb of the Roman Empire. Roman soldiers occupied its land and harassed its people. The Roman government demanded taxes, which the Jewish people were obliged to pay. The Israelites were so desperate to be free from Roman control that they awaited a Messiah who would lead them in a revolt. They assumed this Messiah would be a military figure who would rule over Israel after it regained its independence.

The humble carpenter's son from the backwater village of Nazareth fulfilled exactly none of their expectations. Just as Isaiah had predicted, there was nothing in Jesus's appearance that would attract people to Him (Isa. 53:2). He didn't look like the public perception of a Messiah.

Jesus didn't go out of His way to ingratiate Himself with the Pharisees. He didn't play the political games of the Sadducees. He wasn't impressed by the Jewish religious leaders' rule-following. He saw the hypocrisy in the way they neglected justice, mercy, and faithfulness as they nitpicked over minutiae.

Jesus seemed to prefer blue-collar company—and worse. He surrounded Himself with fishermen. He dined with tax collectors. He treated women and foreigners with respect. He protected an adulteress from a vengeful mob. He took pity on beggars and lepers.

That kind of radicalism put Jesus in the crosshairs of the Pharisees and Sadducees. These men used their religious training and lofty position in Jewish society to try to intimidate Jesus and expose Him as a fraud. And they found they couldn't do it.

In the Gospels, these esteemed scholars come off looking like Wile E. Coyote trying to catch the Road Runner. They laid elaborate verbal traps, trying to get Jesus to say something that was scripturally inaccurate or politically dangerous. And every one of their traps malfunctioned, usually capturing them instead. They desperately tried to find fault in Jesus, only to have their efforts boomerang back on them and expose their own faults.

Jesus understood what the Jewish religious leaders could not fathom: His coming marked the end of the law—the system of commandments and sacrifices the leaders had built their lives on. His sinless life would end the pursuit of righteousness through rule-following. His sacrificial death would negate the need for any further sacrifices. Jesus brought the law of Moses to a close by fulfilling every bit of it. It was the surprise ending virtually no one saw coming.

To those who expected an earthly warrior-king, Jesus said, "My kingdom is not of this world" (John 18:36). The revolution He led was against something far greater than any empire. Jesus came to destroy the power of sin and death, once and for all. No one expected that.

More than two thousand years later, Jesus continues to defy expectations. If we're not careful, we can get lulled into believing we have a pretty good handle on who Jesus is and where He belongs in our lives. We decide which of His teachings are applicable and which ones might raise eyebrows. We think there are some things Jesus can change and some things He can't. We place our own expectations on the Great Defier of expectations.

Jesus Suffered

Second, during His time on earth, Jesus suffered. One of the reasons most Jewish people refused to acknowledge Jesus as the Messiah was that He embraced the role of the Suffering Servant, prophesied in Isaiah 53. Jewish leaders certainly were aware of Isaiah's prophecy, but they didn't believe the Messiah and the Suffering Servant would be the same person.

After all, the Messiah was supposed to rule forever. The Suffering Servant had to die. There seemed to be no way to reconcile the two. That's why, when Jesus announced to His disciples that He would suffer, be killed, and then rise from the dead, Peter contradicted Him (Matt. 16:21–22). Jesus's reply was sharp and unyielding. He embraced the role of Suffering Servant. He willingly endured the pain that came with it—not just at the cross but throughout His public ministry.

Jesus suffered verbal attacks on His character, led by some of the most respected people of His time. The religious leaders who opposed Him were blind to the irony of their actions. These men were so reverent in their approach to God the Father that they would not even pronounce His name. Yet when they came face-to-face with God, in the person of

God the Son, they sneered at Him, despised Him, and even accused Him of being possessed by a demon.

Jesus suffered the betrayal of His friends. On the night of His arrest, Jesus ate a final meal with His twelve disciples. Within a few hours, one of them betrayed Him, another denied knowing Him, and the rest ran away.

Jesus suffered the rejection of the people. The crowd who cheered His triumphal entry into Jerusalem on Palm Sunday screamed for His crucifixion five days later. They taunted and jeered at Him as He hung on the cross.

Ah, yes, the cross.

Thousands of years of perfecting the art of torture eventually produced Roman crucifixion. We'll examine the events of Jesus's death in our study of the core belief of salvation. But we need to recognize that the physical agony Jesus experienced on the cross paled in comparison to His spiritual torture. In 2 Corinthians 5:21, Paul said, "[God] made Him who knew no sin to be sin on our behalf." In God's eyes, Jesus became the sins of the world.

Remember the complete perfection of God the Father we talked about in our study of God the Father? Because He is holy, God can have nothing to do with sin, even when that sin is placed on His own Son. As Jesus hung on the cross, God turned away from Him. God the Son experienced an aloneness so profound that it caused Him to cry out.

Jesus could have ended His suffering in an instant. In fact, He could have chosen to avoid it altogether. He willingly endured it because the penalty for our sins had to be paid. But there was another reason as well.

Grief counselors advise would-be comforters not to use phrases such as "I know how you feel" when offering condolences to hurting people. The words ring hollow because often we *don't* know how they feel. We've never experienced a situation like the one they're going through.

Jesus endured all the suffering this world had to offer so that He could truthfully say to us when we suffer, "I know how you feel." He can empathize with our struggles, our temptations, our feelings of rejection and loneliness, and our physical and emotional pain because He experienced them. He has a fellow sufferer's understanding of when to encourage, how to comfort, and what will bring wholeness. Jesus suffered so that He could counsel and heal us in our suffering.

The writer of Hebrews explained it this way: "Since we have a great high priest who has passed through the heavens, Jesus the Son of God, let us hold fast our confession. For we do not have a high priest who cannot sympathize with our weaknesses, but One who has been tempted in all things as we are, yet without sin. Therefore let us draw near with confidence to the throne of grace, so that we may receive mercy and find grace to help in time of need" (4:14–16).

Jesus Noticed

Third, during His time on earth, Jesus noticed. He paid attention to the world around Him. He saw spiritual truths in everything from a mustard seed to the birds of the air to a barren fig tree. He crafted parables and teachings to help others notice too.

Jesus saw the outcasts who slipped through the cracks of society. He recognized the value of men and women others called worthless. As Jesus was leaving the city of Jericho, a blind beggar named Bartimaeus cried out, "Jesus, Son of

DID JESUS CLAIM TO BE THE MESSIAH?

Some people say Jesus was an influential philosopher and a moral teacher but nothing more. They claim Jesus never identified Himself as the Son of God, Messiah, or Savior—that those titles were given to Him by His exaggeration-prone disciples.

However, those arguments are hard to defend when passages like these are in the Bible:

- The woman at the well said, "I know that Messiah is coming (He who is called Christ); when that One comes, He will declare all things to us." Jesus answered, "I who speak to you am He" (John 4:25-26).
- Jesus said, "I and the Father are one" (John 10:30).
- The high priest said to Jesus, "I adjure You by the living God, that You tell us whether You are the Christ, the Son of God." Jesus replied, "You have said it yourself" (Matt. 26:63-64).

David, have mercy on me!" The crowd around him tried to silence the beggar, but Bartimaeus refused to stay quiet. Jesus stopped and healed him (Mark 10:46–52).

Mark 5:24–34 tells the story of a woman who had suffered from a blood disorder for twelve years. Too timid to call out to Jesus as Bartimaeus had done, she quietly touched Jesus's cloak, hoping to be healed without bothering the Healer. To her amazement, she discovered that she was not a bother to Him at all. She was a priority.

Jesus spotted the real needs, motivations, and potential in the people He encountered. He gathered around Him a small group of fishermen, religious seekers, women who were accustomed to being treated as second-class citizens, and others on the fringes of society. He saw in them the potential for extraordinary courage, wisdom, commitment, and ingenuity. He entrusted them with His message, knowing they could—and would—change the world with it.

Jesus calls us to be noticers as well. Our daily lives are packed full of God's blessings, just waiting to be recognized. The natural world shouts testimony of our Creator's perfect design, provision, and love for us. All we have to do is pay attention. Jesus calls us to be "shrewd as serpents and innocent as doves" (Matt. 10:16). That wisdom involves being able to see past people's exteriors and recognize their true needs and motivations. The impact we have on others' lives, in showing them Christ's love, begins with three simple words: *I see you.*

What Did Jesus Prioritize?

Jesus's time on earth was brief, as He knew it would be. The time He spent in the public eye was even briefer. So His priorities—the things He chose to focus on during that time—speak volumes. They show all of us who follow Him what we should be focusing on.

His Father's Word

First, Jesus prioritized His Father's Word. More than anyone, Jesus understood the potential of God's Word. Luke 2:52 summarizes Jesus's adolescence by saying He "kept increasing in wisdom and stature, and in favor with God and men." In the story that precedes that verse, we see evidence of His increasing wisdom. When Jesus's parents couldn't locate Him during their journey home from Jerusalem after the Passover celebration, they returned to the city and found Him in the temple. Luke 2:47 says Jesus amazed the teachers there with His understanding—the kind of knowledge that comes from diligent study.

Long before Paul used the image of a sword to depict the Word of God as part of a Christian's spiritual armor (Eph. 6:17), Jesus used it as a defensive spiritual weapon. Matthew 4 describes how Satan appeared to Jesus in the wilderness to try to coax Him into abandoning His earthly mission. Satan presented three tempting scenarios that would have allowed Jesus to claim earthly glory without pain and suffering.

In the Marvel Comics or Star Wars universes, a showdown like that, between ultimate good and ultimate evil, would feature landscape-altering energy pulses and lightning bolts shooting from fingertips. Jesus opted for a more powerful weapon. Every time Satan presented a temptation, Jesus countered by quoting Scripture. Satan was powerless against it. The third time Jesus quoted it, Satan left Him. We need to understand that God's Word has lost none of its power to defeat Satan and his schemes since then.

His Father's Presence

Second, Jesus prioritized His Father's presence. Throughout Jesus's ministry, He showed us how to draw strength from God's companionship. Though He was often surrounded by crowds, He remained unaffected by their demands. He didn't seek popularity. The only approval Jesus needed was His Father's. And He always had it. Their relationship is best captured in the words God the Father spoke at Jesus's baptism: "This is My beloved Son, in whom I am well-pleased" (Matt. 3:17).

God's companionship made Jesus's life and work on earth possible. Sure, Jesus was surrounded by family and friends. He felt their love and support. But they couldn't understand Him the way His heavenly Father could. They couldn't fathom why He said and did certain things. The result of that disconnect was that Jesus had a need for connection, understanding, and fellowship that even His closest family members and friends couldn't provide.

So Jesus did what anyone who feels a similar disconnect can do: He turned to His heavenly Father—early, often, and purposefully. According to Luke 5:16, "Jesus Himself would often slip away to the wilderness and pray."

Mark 1 gives us a fuller picture of Jesus's quiet times with God: "In the early morning, while it was still dark, Jesus got up, left the house, and went away to a secluded place, and was praying there. Simon and his companions searched for Him; they found Him, and said to Him, 'Everyone is looking for You'" (vv. 35–37).

Jesus needed time with His heavenly Father more than He needed sleep. He needed a place free of distractions so that He could focus on talking to God, listening to Him, and being in His presence. He refused to allow the pressing needs of the day or the agendas of others to cut into His quiet time. He stayed alone in God's presence until He was ready to begin His day. Jesus's time with God prepared Him to do what God had in store for Him.

His Father's Will

Third, Jesus prioritized His Father's will. In John 4, Jesus's companions grew concerned that His ministry to others was causing Him to neglect His own basic needs. "The disciples were urging Him, saying, 'Rabbi, eat.' But He said to them, 'I have food to eat that you do not know about.' So the disciples were saying to one another, 'No one brought Him anything to eat, did he?' Jesus said to them, 'My food is to do the will of Him who sent Me and to accomplish His work'" (vv. 31–34).

What an amazing perspective. Jesus didn't see God's will as the great spoiler of fun. Instead, Jesus embraced God's will as the only real essential in His life. He understood that all His other needs would be provided for as long as He pursued His Father's will.

If you've ever worked a maze puzzle—a really hard one, not one of those obvious, beginner-level ones—you know there are routes that look really promising, sometimes for long stretches, but eventually lead to dead ends. You know the frustration of having to retrace your path, looking for the place where you took a wrong turn. Or, worse, having to start over.

Jesus approached God's will as a previously solved maze puzzle, one that shows the exact route to take. It's not a direct route. The best maze adventures never are. It will wind in ways that don't always make sense to us. Sometimes it will seem as though we're heading into places where there's nothing but dead ends. Then we'll see a path we hadn't considered before, and it will lead us out. At the end of this maze, which we call life, is a place of ultimate fulfillment and joy.

How do we nurture such a healthy attitude toward God's will? We follow Jesus's example of prioritizing quiet time with God. The more time we spend in God's presence—reading and praying about His Word, listening to His voice, and deepening our relationship with Him—the more clearly we will see His will for what it is.

Jesus AD

We saw earlier that Jesus came at a fraught time in Israel's history. But He also came at an ideal time. The Pax Romana, or Roman peace, meant there was no existential threat for people to worry about. They had the luxury of being able to focus on spiritual matters. The intricate road system the Romans built facilitated the spreading of the gospel. Most of the people in the world spoke the same language, Koine Greek, which made sharing the gospel and writing the New Testament much easier. The polytheism, or worship of many gods, that had been a part of Roman and Greek culture was giving way to a renewed interest in monotheism, the worship of one God. And four hundred years of spiritual drought among the Jewish people was coming to an end as a renewed interest in Scripture was starting to take hold.

The stage was set.

God's perfect timing ensured that Jesus's message would resonate, travel, and transform. The movement that started in a small village in occupied Israel more than two thousand years ago changed the world like nothing else before or since.

That's the big-picture view of Jesus's work after His life on earth. What's more important is the practical application:

what His life means for us today. God the Son, the third core belief of Christianity, presents us with two unique opportunities and challenges.

Jesus Presents Us with a Decision to Make

Some people believe Tom Hanks is the greatest actor in Hollywood. Some people believe James Buchanan is the worst president in US history. Both statements make for interesting conversation starters. In certain circles, they might even trigger spirited debate. Ultimately, though, it doesn't really matter how we respond. There are no consequences for our belief or unbelief.

At the opposite end of the consequence spectrum, we have this quote from Jesus: "I am the way, and the truth, and the life; no one comes to the Father but through Me" (John 14:6). Spiritually speaking, that puts the ball in our court.

As Paul explained in Colossians 1:15–20, Jesus has proven Himself to be sufficient for us. Paul was writing to Christians who were tempted to believe that Jesus was not enough, that they needed something else: Jesus plus good works. Jesus plus the Old Testament law. Jesus plus a certain philosophy.

Paul reminded the Colossians of Jesus's credentials: Jesus existed before the world was made. He created the universe. The wind and waves obey Him. He sustains the universe. He holds everything together and keeps it from spinning into chaos.

Paul explained that Jesus was and is the head of the church. He is the "firstborn from the dead" (v. 18)—the first person to be raised in a new body that was free from sin, that would never grow sick or die. The Greek word for "firstborn" (*prototokos*) is the word from which we get our English word *prototype.* Our resurrected bodies will be modeled on Jesus's resurrected body.

Paul pointed out that Jesus is central to salvation. Through Him, God reconciled us to Himself. With our sin, we made a unilateral decision to leave our relationship with Him. We chased after other things and other people. God would have been completely justified in ending His relationship with us. He could have said, "You want to be separated from Me? Why not go ahead, then, and spend the rest of eternity separated from Me?" That would have been a just decision. But God loves us too much for that to happen. He took the first step toward reconciliation by sending His Son to die for us (Rom. 5:8). Jesus made it possible for us to have peace with God. His death was sufficient payment for our sins.

Paul's point was this: if Jesus Christ is sufficient to create and sustain the universe, to deliver us from the power of death, and to restore our relationship with God, don't you think He's sufficient to entrust with our lives?

Jesus's statement is unequivocal: *I am the way.* His résumé gives us no reason to doubt Him. We must decide whether to accept His truth—to embrace it and build our lives on it—or to reject it. And from God's perspective, any response other than fully accepting it is rejecting it.

Jesus Presents Us with a Future to Embrace

Putting our faith in God the Son opens a new future to us and unlocks a new perspective on the world around us. As we wrap up this look at the third core belief of Christianity, let's consider three things that happen when we align ourselves forever with Jesus Christ.

First, *we accept that we're only travelers in this world.* If you've enjoyed an extended stay in a foreign locale, you know the sense of dislocation that can set in. No matter how hard you work to embrace local customs, you're still a foreigner. You don't quite belong, not like the citizens of that region. Your citizenship lies elsewhere.

Paul said that, as Christians, "our citizenship is in heaven" (Phil. 3:20). That makes this world our foreign locale. That realization creates both an opportunity and a responsibility for us. The opportunity is knowing that everything we experience and endure in this world is temporary, a drop in the bucket of eternity. Knowing that there's an end to our struggles can give us the perspective we need to thrive in the midst of them.

On the flip side, because of the temporary nature of this world, we have no reason to get too attached to the things in it, especially if they interfere with our walk with Christ. We have to guard against getting bogged down by earthly pursuits when there are so many opportunities to pursue things of eternal significance.

Second, *we put our treasure in things above.* Figuratively speaking, we look at life through a jeweler's loupe. An experienced jeweler isn't dazzled by a diamond's sparkly exterior. Instead, she examines the stone closely, with a neutral gaze. By looking through a loupe, she's able to see tiny cracks in the surface of the diamond, as well as blemishes and imperfections that are invisible to the naked eye. She gets a sense of the diamond's true value.

Likewise, with a Christlike perspective, we can see the cracks and imperfections in the things of this world that are considered valuable. Popularity is fleeting. Money doesn't buy happiness. Power corrupts. Comfort is a trap.

We can also spot the things that *are* truly valuable. Serving others changes lives. Studying God's Word pays enormous dividends. Pursuing His will for our lives results in ultimate fulfillment and joy.

Third, *we experience the beautiful tension Paul talked about.* In his letter to Philippian believers, Paul said, "For to me, to live is Christ and to die is gain. But if I am to live on in the flesh, this will mean fruitful labor for me; and I do not know which to choose. But I am hard-pressed from both directions, having the desire to depart and be with Christ, for that is very much better; yet to remain on in the flesh is more necessary for your sake" (1:21–24).

On the one hand, we eagerly anticipate the things we can do for God on earth and celebrate the blessings we experience here. On the other hand, we recognize that the glory that awaits us in heaven is far greater than anything we could ever hope to experience here on earth.

In other words, we celebrate the win-win of our existence—the existence made possible by God the Son.

4

GOD THE HOLY SPIRIT

Are you familiar with the "rule of three"? Maybe you haven't heard it referred to by name, but you're likely familiar with the idea. If you've ever watched a movie or TV show, you've seen it at work. Almost all screenplays and scripts have a three-act structure. So do most public presentations. You'll find that the best sermons, motivational speeches, and sales pitches contain three points. Three is substantive enough to convey the importance of a message and succinct enough to make it memorable. The principle applies to informal communication as well. When someone is telling a joke, how many guys invariably walk into a bar?

Interior designers have found that arrangements of three—picture frames, artwork, furniture groupings—are especially pleasing to the eye. Some of the best-loved musical groups of all time had three members.

Yet there's an interesting twist to this three-mania. Often when things are arranged in triads, one assumes a complementary role. One recedes slightly to emphasize the other two. Sometimes that receding is a purposeful strategy, as in a musical arrangement. Sometimes it happens naturally, and unfairly, as part of human psychology.

Think vanilla in Neapolitan ice cream, yellow in a stoplight, and Larry in the Three Stooges. The receding member is equally as important as the other two members of the trio, just not as prominent.

With that in mind, let's examine the fourth core belief of Christianity, God the Holy Spirit. The name is a giveaway. But in light of our three-centric introduction, it bears repeating: the Holy Spirit is God, just as God the Father is God and God the Son is God.

If the Holy Spirit sometimes seems to recede in comparison to the other two persons of the Trinity, it's due only to our limited perspective. The role of God the Father is prominent in our daily routine and conversation. We begin our prayers with "Dear heavenly Father." We celebrate His love for us. We strive to do His will. The role of God the Son is equally prominent. Jesus is the Word, the Messiah, the Savior, the Prince of Peace, the Lamb of God, our High Priest, the King of kings and Lord of lords.

The Holy Spirit's role, in contrast, is not quite as high-profile in our Christian culture. For many believers, He's like the key grip or head gaffer in movie credits. We know He does important work; we're just not sure what it is. The fact that He always receives third billing in the Trinity may cause some people to underestimate His importance.

The reality is that there is no aspect of the Christian life that doesn't require the Holy Spirit's assistance. The more we understand about who He is, what He's done, and what He continues to do, the more purposeful we will become in drawing on His power in our own lives.

Studying the Holy Spirit's Résumé

The perfections of God the Holy Spirit are the same as those we identified in God the Father and God the Son. The Holy Spirit is eternal. There has never been a time when He didn't exist. The Holy Spirit is also perfectly holy, just, loving, eternal, all-powerful, all-knowing, immanent, transcendent, sovereign, and unchanging.

You won't find the Holy Spirit mentioned in the first verse of the Bible. But you will find Him in the second verse: "The

THE TRINITY: IN 120 WORDS OR LESS

God the Father is God. God the Son is God. God the Holy Spirit is God. Add them together and you get . . . one. How is that possible? Therein lies the challenge of explaining the Trinity.

God is one (Deut. 6:4). However, within His oneness, He makes Himself known in three different persons: Father, Son, and Holy Spirit. Each person in the Trinity has unique responsibilities, but no person acts independently of the others. All three are always in complete agreement and unity. They are also equal. No person is more important than the others. The Holy Spirit's work is every bit as essential as that of God the Father and God the Son.

Spirit of God was moving over the surface of the waters" (Gen. 1:2). As the physical universe was being spoken into existence, the Holy Spirit was right there, making it happen. His creative power brought order out of chaos. The book of Job tells us the Holy Spirit played an even more personal role in creation. In Job 33:4, Elihu said, "The Spirit of God has made me, and the breath of the Almighty gives me life." One breath from the Holy Spirit gave life to the entire human race.

Countless other Old Testament passages confirm that the Holy Spirit stayed close to His breath-carriers. In fact, He involved Himself in the lives of His people in extraordinary ways. In the book of Judges, the phrase "the Spirit of the LORD came upon" appears again and again. The results of His coming speak for themselves. The Spirit of the Lord came upon Othniel, and he rescued the Israelites from the hands of an evil king (Judg. 3:10). The Spirit of the Lord came upon Gideon—a man who, by his own admission, was the least-renowned member of the weakest family in his tribe (6:34). Yet after the Spirit came upon him, this "nobody" led the Israelites to an unforgettable military victory over the Midianites. The Spirit of the Lord came upon Samson, and he wreaked havoc on the Philistines—using the supernatural strength that had been given to him—until his dying breath (15:14).

Othniel, Gideon, and Samson hold special places in the history of God's people. And when it was time for them to fulfill their role in God's plan, the Holy Spirit came alongside them to make sure they were equipped for the task. Their power came from the Holy Spirit, and their success was due to Him.

THE DEPARTING OF THE HOLY SPIRIT

"The Spirit of the LORD departed from Saul" (1 Sam. 16:14). This departure was devastating to Saul, but it's no cause for alarm for believers today. Saul, like other leaders in the Old Testament, was anointed and empowered by the Holy Spirit to fulfill his God-given calling to govern the people of Israel. But when Saul disobeyed, the Spirit departed from him, and Saul lost his empowerment. His governing responsibilities were taken away from him. The Holy Spirit came upon him temporarily and left him when the situation dictated.

But things have changed dramatically since then—since Pentecost in Acts 2, to be more precise. Today, the Holy Spirit indwells every believer, fully and permanently, the moment we are saved. He will not depart from us. We cannot lose Him.

King David voiced a different perspective on the Holy Spirit's work and presence during perhaps the lowest point of his life. David committed adultery with Bathsheba, the wife of one of his noblest warriors. When Bathsheba became pregnant, David arranged for her husband to be killed so that he could marry her and make the pregnancy seem legitimate. (The details of his sordid plan are in 2 Samuel 11:1–12:25.)

In the wake of these sins, David understandably felt distant from the Lord. In Psalm 51:11, he begged God not to remove the Holy Spirit from his life. David understood that without the Holy Spirit's guidance, he had no chance of knowing, much less following, God's will for his life. The

Holy Spirit makes it possible for us to live God-honoring lives.

Passages such as Ezekiel 2:2 ("the Spirit entered me and . . . I heard Him speaking to me") identify the Holy Spirit as the one who revealed God's truth to the Old Testament prophets and prompted them to write down what they heard. The apostle Paul also acknowledged the Holy Spirit's role in revealing God's prophecy when he said, "The Holy Spirit rightly spoke through Isaiah the prophet to your fathers" (Acts 28:25). Because all prophecy in Scripture was initiated by the Holy Spirit, we can put our faith in it as being trustworthy.

In fact, the same goes for all of Scripture. The apostle Peter made it clear that the Holy Spirit superintended the writing of the Bible. The authors of the individual books didn't decide what to write; they relied on the inspiration of the Holy Spirit (2 Pet. 1:20–21).

The Spirit's work in the New Testament began with Mary's conception. Luke 1:35 tells us that the Holy Spirit caused the mother of Jesus to conceive her "holy Child." Going back to His role in biblical prophecy, that means the Holy Spirit announced through Isaiah that the Savior would be born of a virgin and then, seven hundred years later, He made it possible for that prophecy to be fulfilled.

After Jesus was born, the Spirit worked in ministry support for thirty-three years. During Jesus's earthly life, the Holy Spirit provided Him with strength, comfort, encouragement, and companionship. The Spirit gave Jesus what His human friends could not.

The spotlight shifts briefly in John 14:16–17 as Jesus calmed His disciples' fears about what would happen to them after

He returned to heaven. His message, in so many words, was this: "You won't be alone when I leave, because God the Father is going to send another Helper who will be with you forever. You may mourn now, but when this Helper comes, you're going to be glad you have Him."

The disciples didn't have to wait long for Jesus's "parting gift" to come. A matter of days after Jesus ascended to heaven, the Holy Spirit arrived in miraculous fashion in Jerusalem, where Jesus's followers were gathered to celebrate Pentecost. And thus began the Holy Spirit's personal work in the lives of all believers. (We will explore the Holy Spirit's work at Pentecost in more detail when we study the core belief of the church.)

Appreciating the Holy Spirit's Work

The personal work of the Holy Spirit not only impacts virtually every area of our daily lives but also shapes our identity as believers. Let's look at just a few of the things the Holy Spirit accomplishes in the world today.

The Holy Spirit Dwells in Every Believer

Think about the power of God that flung billions of galaxies into existence with a single word, that changed five loaves and two fish into enough food to feed more than five thousand people, and that lifted Jesus Christ out of His grave. Did you know that same power is in you and me right now, if we trust in Christ as our Savior?

What an amazing, exhilarating realization! After all, we all feel the need for more power in our lives, don't we? We need more power in our prayers. We need more power in saying no to sin. We need more power to be courageous. We need more power to find peace when our world is collapsing around us. And, as Christians, we have it. The power we possess is not a special force but a person: the Holy Spirit.

Unfortunately, far too many Christians go through life unaware of the great, supernatural power of the Holy Spirit within them. But the Holy Spirit is there, whether we choose to access His power or not. The Holy Spirit takes up residence within every person who accepts Christ as Savior. He is not optional equipment; He is the basic package for every believer.

In 2 Peter 1:3–4, Peter said, "His divine power has granted to us everything pertaining to life and godliness, through the true knowledge of Him who called us by His own glory and excellence. For by these He has granted to us His precious and magnificent promises, so that by them you may become partakers of the divine nature, having escaped the corruption that is in the world by lust."

Pay particular attention to the phrase "His divine power has granted to us everything pertaining to life and godliness." If we are Christians, God has not shortchanged us. God isn't reserving something extra that we need to beg Him for or ask Him to do in our lives. He has given you and me everything we need to lead a supernaturally fulfilling existence. He has given us everything pertaining to life and godliness. And everything He has given us is wrapped up in the Holy Spirit.

The Holy Spirit Makes Us Aware of Sin

The Holy Spirit's work goes hand in hand with His dwelling in us. Because of His nearness, He feels our sin deeply.

In fact, when we sin, we take the Holy Spirit along for the ride. Remember, He's in us; He isn't going anywhere. He has an uncomfortably close perspective on our wrongdoing. That's why Paul said in Ephesians 4:30, "Do not grieve the Holy Spirit of God, by whom you were sealed for the day of redemption."

The Holy Spirit acts as our spiritual conscience, letting us know when we sin and urging us to repent (John 16:8). Anytime we feel pangs of guilt or regret—anytime we sin and feel the need to ask God for forgiveness—we know that the Holy Spirit is at work.

Without the Spirit's insistent prompting, we would be in trouble. Our own moral compass is faulty. Our ability to rationalize, justify, and downplay our wrongdoings makes us incapable of accurately gauging our spiritual condition. We can walk around blissfully unaware of the damage that our sin is doing to us, to others, and especially to our relationship with God.

The result of the Holy Spirit's convicting work in our lives is a closer relationship to the Lord. Sin interferes with our relationship with God. So by keeping us informed of our sin and prompting us to confess it, the Holy Spirit works to ensure that we don't drift away from God and His plan for our lives.

The Holy Spirit Amplifies Our Prayers

The Holy Spirit makes prayer possible—life-transforming, God-honoring, world-altering prayer. He does it by translating our human utterances into the adoration, confession, thanksgiving, and supplication that please God and draw His blessing.

Paul gave us some hints as to how this work takes place in Romans 8:26–27: "In the same way the Spirit also helps our weakness; for we do not know how to pray as we should, but the Spirit Himself intercedes for us with groanings too deep for words; and He who searches the hearts knows what the mind of the Spirit is, because He intercedes for the saints according to the will of God." In other words, the Holy Spirit "fills in" our prayers, taking needs before the Lord that we're unable to express—or that we may not even be aware of.

The Holy Spirit Distributes Spiritual Gifts

When we were born into this world physically, we were born with certain natural abilities. Some people have the ability to play an instrument. Others have the ability to sing. Some have the ability to work with their hands. Some have leadership abilities. These are all natural gifts.

When we were born again into the family of God, the Holy Spirit brought into each of our lives a spiritual gift, which is both a desire and a unique power to be a part of God's ministry. In 1 Corinthians 12:4–11, the apostle Paul described the source and purpose of our spiritual gifts. He explained, "One and the same Spirit works all these things, distributing to each one individually just as He wills" (v. 11). The Holy Spirit decides what gift we receive, and we are to use our spiritual gifts "for the common good" (v. 7).

To some Christians, the Holy Spirit gives the gift of prophecy—not in the sense of foretelling the future but the ability to speak God's Word with conviction. He gives some people the gift of mercy, the ability to empathize with the sorrows of others. He gives some people the gift of giving, the unique ability to multiply financial assets and use them for God's kingdom purposes. He gives some people the gift of spiritual leadership. (For more spiritual gifts, see Romans 12:6–8 and Ephesians 4:11–12.)

Every Christian has a spiritual gift. It's no accident that the Greek word translated as "gift" has at its root a word that means "joy." Nothing gives Christians more joy than discovering and using their spiritual gifts—realizing that God has empowered them in a unique way to be a part of His kingdom purpose. The Holy Spirit connects us to God's eternal purpose by imparting to us a unique spiritual gift when we're saved.

The Holy Spirit Reveals the Deep Things of God

The Holy Spirit can understand what we never can: the thoughts of God Himself. "Who among men knows the thoughts of a man except the spirit of the man which is in him? Even so the thoughts of God no one knows except the Spirit of God" (1 Cor. 2:11).

Without the Holy Spirit, we would have no hope of comprehending the way God works. Our finite minds are insufficient tools for grasping infinite concepts. The Holy Spirit reveals God's thoughts to us because He loves us and wants what's best for us.

The Holy Spirit also reveals God's Word to us. But He does it in conjunction with our study of the Bible. He doesn't just download the wisdom of the ages into our brains the moment we give our lives to Christ. Instead, He rewards our efforts to understand God's Word. When we dig into Scripture, He guides us to treasure.

The Holy Spirit Fosters Unity in the Church

How does the Holy Spirit foster unity in the church? Paul said to look in the mirror. Look at your body. You're not one giant ear or one giant eyeball or one giant nostril. Your body consists of a variety of different parts, yet those parts all function together for the same purpose.

That's the way the church is to be. Look at 1 Corinthians 12:12: "For even as the body is one and yet has many members, and all the members of the body, though they are many, are one body, so also is Christ." Like the human body, the church is made up of many different parts—many kinds of people—all joined together for one purpose. And the way the church comes together from diverse backgrounds to be one is through the baptism of the Holy Spirit.

WHAT IS THE BAPTISM OF THE HOLY SPIRIT?

The word "baptized" that Paul used in 1 Corinthians 12:13 is a transliteration of the Greek word *baptizo*, which means "to immerse." The word was used in classical Greek literature to describe the process of changing the color of cloth. If you wanted to change a red piece of cloth to purple, you would *baptizo* it in a vat of purple dye. You had to immerse it to change its color.

Water baptism is a symbol of what the Holy Spirit does for us when we trust in Christ as our Savior. He immerses us. He transforms us from guilty, rebellious enemies of God into forgiven, obedient disciples of Jesus Christ. He changes our spiritual color forever.

In verse 13, Paul explained the process by which the Holy Spirit sets up residence in every believer's life: "For by one Spirit we were all baptized into one body, whether Jews or Greeks, whether slaves or free, and we were all made to drink of one Spirit."

The baptism of the Holy Spirit is a one-time act of God by which, at the moment of our salvation, the Holy Spirit joins us to Jesus Christ, the head, and to all the other members of the body. Every true Christian has experienced the baptism of the Holy Spirit of God. The moment you become a Christian, you receive all of the Holy Spirit. There's no more of the Holy Spirit for you to receive as a Christian. You've received every part of Him.

Every Christian has been baptized by the Spirit into the body of Christ. But not all Christians are filled with the Spirit, which—as we will see in a moment—is a continual process of choosing to give the Holy Spirit control over your life.

The Holy Spirit Gives Us the Ability to Trust in Christ

Everyone in the world is free to trust in Christ. Jesus said, "Let the one who is thirsty come; let the one who wishes take the water of life without cost" (Rev. 22:17). However, not everyone is willing or able to trust in Christ. If that distinction seems a little fuzzy, consider this analogy. If you set a bale of hay in front of a lion, the lion is free to eat the hay. However, the lion is not willing to eat the hay. The lion is, by nature, a carnivore. There is nothing inside it that desires the hay.

The same principle applies to unbelievers. Unbelievers are free to trust in Christ, but because of their nature—because they are enemies of God—they will never do so. We were all born into this world hating God. Paul underscored that point in Romans 3:10–11: "There is none righteous, not even one; there is none who understands, there is none who seeks for God."

To make matters worse, we were born spiritually dead. Ephesians 2:1 says, "You were dead in your trespasses and sins." While we're free to come to Christ, we're unable to. We can't just wake up spiritually one day and say, "You know what? I'm a sinner and I need a Savior, so I'm going to trust in Christ." It doesn't happen that way.

So if we're all by nature unwilling and unable to come to Christ, how is anybody ever saved? The answer is the Holy Spirit. In Ephesians 2:4–5, Paul said, "God, being rich in mercy, because of His great love with which He loved us, even when we were dead in our transgressions, made us alive together with Christ (by grace you have been saved)." The way God transforms someone who is spiritually dead into being spiritually alive so that he or she wants to and is capable of trusting in Christ is by the Holy Spirit.

The Holy Spirit is the one who gives us the ability to believe and have new life. Our salvation has absolutely nothing to do with us and everything to do with God. Even our ability to believe is a gift from God. The proper response to that realization is to fall on our knees before God and thank Him that, in His mercy and grace, He saved us.

The Holy Spirit Secures Our Future

Once you've trusted in Christ, how do you know that you'll keep on trusting in Him? How do you know that when you die, God will do what He promised to do and take your spirit to be with Him? How do you know that you are truly a child of God? The answer to all those questions is the Holy Spirit.

The Holy Spirit's presence within us is our Christian birth certificate, the way to prove we're legitimate children of God. In Ephesians 1:13–14, Paul used two words to describe how the Holy Spirit secures our future: "In Him, you also, after listening to the message of truth, the gospel of your salvation— having also believed, you were *sealed* in Him with the Holy Spirit of promise, who is given as a *pledge* of our inheritance, with a view to the redemption of God's own possession, to the praise of His glory."

Seals were an early form of notarization. Today if we need to authenticate a document, we take it to a notary. The notary takes out a special seal, presses it on the document to create an insignia, charges us a fee, and then sends us on our way. In Paul's day, a notary official wore a ring that had the insignia of the king or emperor on it. Notarizing a document was done by pressing the ring onto a circle of hot wax on the document. When the wax cooled, the document bore the imprint of the king or emperor. Sealing a document in this manner showed its authenticity.

That's the image Paul used in this passage. He said, in effect, "When you trust in Christ as your Savior, the King of kings marks you with an imprint of Himself." And that seal is the Holy Spirit. God stamps us with His image, guaranteeing that we are truly His children.

The Holy Spirit also serves as a pledge of our future inheritance. The Greek word translated as "pledge" literally means "down payment." The Holy Spirit's presence in our lives is God's down payment on His future fulfillment of

His promise to us. One day He's going to take our spirits to be with Him forever. One day He's going to raise our bodies out of the ground. In the meantime, He gives us His Holy Spirit to show His earnestness in completing His deal with us.

In offering the Holy Spirit as a down payment, God isn't giving us some paltry fraction of Himself. Instead, when we become Christians, God invests 100 percent of Himself in us through the Holy Spirit. Do you think God is going to turn His back on that investment? Do you think He's going to walk away from the deal? Not on your life. Because God has invested all of Himself in us, one day He's going to consummate the deal. One day He's going to take our spirits to heaven, just as He promised. One day He's going to raise our bodies from the dead and change them forever, just as He promised. The Holy Spirit is God's pledge that secures our future.

Accessing the Holy Spirit's Power

If all Christians are indwelled by the Holy Spirit, then why do so many of us struggle to maintain a consistent prayer life? Why do we have at least one bad habit (or addiction) we can't break? Why do we have difficulty controlling our thoughts and actions?

More to the point, why are some Christians able to rise above those struggles? Why do they have the power to say no to sin? Why do they have joy, no matter what's happening around them? Why do they seem to get more yes than no answers to their prayers? Why do they seem to be more filled with the Spirit? Why are they able to access His power?

The phrase "filled with the Spirit" is used fifteen times in the New Testament. The Greek word translated as "filled" refers to the wind that fills the sails of a ship and controls its direction. For believers, to be filled with the Spirit means that God's Spirit controls the direction of our lives.

In Ephesians 5:18, Paul said, "Do not get drunk with wine, for that is dissipation, but be filled with the Spirit." In this short verse, we find two essential truths about being filled with the Holy Spirit. First, being filled with the Holy Spirit is a command, not a promise. Being controlled by the Holy Spirit is our responsibility, not God's. Imagine that someone says something that really ticks you off. Your first reaction may be to unleash a few choice words. But an inner prompting says, *If you do that, you'll regret it. Keep your cool.* You have a choice. Will you be controlled by anger or by the Spirit?

Second, being filled with the Spirit is a continual experience, not a one-time action. Picture a sailboat crossing the ocean. The wind doesn't come one time and fill the sails for the entire journey. It comes for a while, leaves, and comes back again. It may even change direction. The same goes for the filling of the Holy Spirit. The command in Ephesians 5:18 could be translated as "keep on being filled with the Spirit."

There is no one-time prayer that will forever free us from our struggle with sin. However, the struggle gets easier the more often we choose to be filled with the Spirit. Making that choice is a habit we develop. The payoffs of developing that habit, of learning to surrender to the control of the Holy Spirit, are life-changing. The Holy Spirit gives us power in times of temptation, direction in times of confusion, courage in times of opportunity, and comfort in times of stress.

Four Conduits of the Holy Spirit's Power

How do we receive the power of the Holy Spirit's filling? Scripture indicates that there are four main conduits He uses to energize us.

The first conduit is the Bible. The Spirit of God uses the Word of God to unleash the power of God to transform us into the image of God. In Psalm 119:105, David said, "Your word is a lamp to my feet and a light to my path." Through Scripture, the Holy Spirit gives us just the amount of illumination we need to take our next step. And then the next step. And then the step after that. The problem is, many Christians have that light turned off. They have it lying on a shelf somewhere. They're stumbling around in the dark, wondering why they don't receive the guidance they need to make the right decisions.

The second conduit is prayer. Throughout both the Old and New Testaments, we see God's power being poured out on His people through prayer. Prayer caused the fire of God to consume Elijah's offering on Mount Carmel. Prayer allowed Jesus to feed thousands of people miraculously. That same power is available to us.

The third conduit is the church. Acts 2:42–47 gives us a glimpse of the Spirit's power in action in a local congregation. This passage describes believers continually devoting themselves to teaching, fellowship, and prayer. These believers felt a sense of awe at what was taking place in and through them. Not only did they experience gladness and sincerity of heart, but they also made an indelible impact on others. The Lord added to their number daily, as more and more people saw the tangible benefits of coming to Christ.

They were, as the writer of Hebrews put it, stimulating one another to love and good deeds (10:24–25). They were also combining their spiritual gifts to great effect, learning from one another how to be generous, encouraging, merciful, and comforting. The same opportunities await us in the church today. (We will explore this more in our study of the core belief of the church.)

The fourth conduit is obedience to God. Obedience helps us get out of our own way. In 1 Thessalonians 5:19, Paul warned, "Do not quench the Spirit." If we're not careful, we can inadvertently quench the fire of the Holy Spirit in our lives through our actions.[1]

Immorality is one such Spirit-quencher. That's why Paul said in 1 Corinthians 6:18, "Flee immorality. Every other sin that a man commits is outside the body, but the immoral man sins against his own body." Immorality includes any sexual activity outside of marriage. Because the Holy Spirit dwells in us, any sin we commit with our body takes Him along.

Bitterness is another Spirit-quencher. It quenches the Spirit's power to heal our hurts. Emotional pain is inevitable in this world. Sooner or later, someone is going to hurt us. We can't do anything about it, but we can control our response to those hurts. We can either hold on to them and allow them to turn into bitterness—or we can forgive the people who hurt us, as God forgives us, and turn those hurts over to Him.

Worry is yet another Spirit-quencher. Did you know that the most common command in Scripture is "Fear not"? It's found 365 times in the Bible. It's as if God is saying to us at least once a day, *Don't be afraid.* How can we keep fear from extinguishing the Spirit's peace in our lives? First, we determine the source of our fear. Is it a prompting from God? Is it the result of fatigue? Is it a lie of Satan? Second, once we determine the source, we confront our fear. We do what we dread. We say what needs to be said. We take the necessary steps to disable our fear. Third, we turn it over to God. We follow the advice of 1 Peter 5:7 and cast all our cares on God. He can shoulder them.

Some time ago, I was flipping through some of my spiritual journals from many years ago. I had written in these journals things I was concerned about, things I was praying for, and, in some cases, things I was fearful about. I started laughing as I read them, because not one of those things I feared a decade or two ago ever happened. Now, other stuff happened that I didn't know about and didn't expect. But nothing I was fearful about ever came to pass. Isn't that just like Satan? He loves to get us overwhelmed by the what-ifs of life, things that will never occur. That's why Jesus said in John 8:44 that Satan is a liar. He's the father of all lies. He wants us to worry about things that have no basis in reality.

The Adventure of Accessing the Holy Spirit's Power

The filling of the Holy Spirit defies conventional wisdom about power in two important ways. First, conventional wisdom says power should be conserved, whether it's electrical, fossil fuel–based, or something else. We're taught to use only as much of it as we absolutely need, that anything more is wasteful and selfish.

The Holy Spirit, on the other hand, encourages us to do the spiritual equivalent of cranking the thermostat to max and putting the pedal to the floor. His power is limitless. He wants us to explore its depths, to access as much of it as we can as often as we can.

Conventional wisdom also teaches us that too much power is dangerous. If we don't keep it under control, bad things can happen. Think of the nuclear power plant in *The China Syndrome* or a race-car driver heading into a turn. The Holy Spirit, in contrast, is not just our power source; He's also behind the wheel. He's in control. We never have to worry when His power is flowing through us.

An unforgettable adventure awaits us if we come to grips with who dwells within us and what He's prepared to do if we will only access His power.

5

ANGELS
AND DEMONS

During the Civil War, most Americans relied on newspapers for information about the conflict. Correspondents accompanied armies into the field and wrote articles based on what they witnessed firsthand and what soldiers reported to them after battles. Sometimes the articles were transmitted to the newspaper office via telegraph. Other times the correspondents had to rely on couriers. By the time the articles were edited, typeset, printed, and delivered via the post office, days and sometimes weeks had passed since the events they described.

Understandably, the time lag in receiving information made the war seem more remote than it actually was. The fact that the bulk of the fighting took place in the South added more perceived distance from the war's realities for people in the North.

That illusion of distance and remoteness lasted just until the war landed in their front yard. After July 3, 1863, no one in Gettysburg, Pennsylvania, would have described the Civil War as a distant conflict.

We face a similar misconception about the cosmic war that's been raging ever since Satan rebelled against God. The apostle Paul, acting as a spiritual battlefield correspondent, said, "Our struggle is not against flesh and blood, but against the rulers, against the powers, against the world forces of this darkness, against the spiritual forces of wickedness in the heavenly places" (Eph. 6:12).

Phrases such as "spiritual forces" and "heavenly places" can lull us into believing this distant conflict has little to do with us. After all, the fighting was going on long before we got here, and it will continue long after we're gone.

But that illusion of distance is shattered when we realize that the battlefield isn't just on our doorstep—it's also *within* us. This titanic spiritual war against the invading armies of darkness and wickedness takes place every minute of every day of our lives. And the rules of the Geneva Convention don't apply.

The stakes couldn't be higher. This is not only a matter of life and death; it's an eternal struggle. To shift our perspective on this cosmic battle so we see it in more personal terms, we need to understand who our angelic allies are, who our demonic enemies are, and how we can apply that understanding to our own battles. When it comes to understanding what the Bible teaches about angels and demons, we need to look at the good, the bad, and the upshot.

The Good—Angels

Angels have gained a curious prominence in our culture. They're like folk heroes who are celebrated for reasons no one can quite put their finger on. Yes, it's true that angels figure in some dramatic moments in Scripture, but only as God directs them. The Bible says that angels are heavenly servants, content to do the will of God forever. Yet today we can find angels in movies, in TV commercials, on product labels, atop Christmas trees, on sports jerseys, in the names of cities, and on countless knickknack shelves.

This fascination with angels is nothing new. In the first-century church at Colossae, there were false teachers who claimed to be too humble to worship God, so they worshiped angels instead (Col. 2:18). And in Revelation 22:8–9, the apostle John fell down at the feet of an angel and started to worship him. But the mortified angel put an immediate stop to it. "Worship God," he said.

To put angels in a proper context, we need to look at what the Bible says about who they are and what they do.

Angels Are Created Beings

Unlike God the Father, God the Son, and God the Holy Spirit, angels are not eternal. They were created by God at a point in time. Referring to Jesus in Colossians 1:16, Paul said, "For by Him *all things* were created, both in the heavens and on earth, visible and invisible, whether thrones or dominions or rulers or authorities—*all things* have been created through Him and for Him." That "all things" includes angels.

Narrowing the timeframe of when angels were created requires a little detective work. In the book of Job, God asked

His long-suffering servant, "Where were you when I laid the foundation of the earth . . . when the morning stars sang together and all the sons of God shouted for joy?" (38:4, 7). We know that God formed the foundation of the earth on the third day of creation (Gen. 1:9–10), so that means the angels had to be in existence by then. Angels were created sometime before the third day of creation.

Angels hold a unique place in creation in that there is a fixed number of them. Some translations of Revelation 5:11, including the NIV, put the number at "ten thousand times ten thousand." Taken literally, that puts the angel population in the hundreds of millions. Other translations use the word "myriad," the highest figure in the Greek system. Whatever the number of angels is, it remains constant, because no new angels have been created since then, and angels never die.

By the way, every angel is a direct creation of God. That is why many times in the Bible angels are called the "sons of God," because each angel was created directly by God. People do not transform into angels when they die. Parents, do not tell your kids they are going to become sweet little cherubs when they die. That is not what the Bible teaches. We do not become angels; we become much better than the angels.

Angels will exist forever—most of them in heaven, praising God. However, the Bible says that fallen angels—those who chose to follow Satan in his rebellion against God—will exist forever in the lake of fire, being tormented day and night. (I'll explain more about these fallen angels in the next section.)

Angels were created with *intellect*. Revelation 10 and 17 suggest that angels know something about God's future.

CHRIST > ANGELS

The writer of Hebrews began his book with a detailed argument about how Jesus is superior to every element of Judaism, starting with angels. He offered four compelling reasons:

1. *Christ has a superior name.* No angel is ever called the unique, begotten Son of God.
2. *Christ is a superior object of worship.* When Jesus came to earth, He didn't worship the angels; the angels worshiped Him.
3. *Christ rules over a superior kingdom.* Hebrews 1:7 says angels are subjects in Christ's kingdom, servants doing His will.
4. *Christ will enjoy a superior victory.* Hebrews 1:13 asks, "But to which of the angels has He [God] ever said, 'Sit at my right hand, until I make Your enemies a footstool for Your feet?'"

Jesus Christ is superior to the angels in every way. One day Jesus will rule over the heavens, the earth, and hell. No angel can ever say that.

Angels were also created with *emotions.* Job 38:7 says they express joy. Isaiah 6:3 says they have the ability to worship. Luke 15:10 says they rejoice when somebody comes to faith in Christ.

Angels were created with a *will.* They have the ability to choose a course of action and follow it. Isaiah 14 describes the most consequential course of action any angel ever chose when Lucifer, God's chief angel—who sinned and then became known as Satan—said, "I will ascend to heaven; I will raise my throne above the stars of God" (v. 13). Five times he said, "I will." Satan made a choice and suffered the consequences for it. Revelation 12:9 indicates that a group of angels chose to follow Satan in his rebellion, and they were cast down to the earth and under it. Their decision was irrevocable. No fallen angel (or demon) will ever be redeemed as a holy angel, and never again will an angel fall and become a demon.

Angels were created as spirit beings, according to Hebrews 1:14. And while angels don't possess bodies, they do share some human limitations, especially when it comes to time and space. Daniel 9:21–23 speaks of angels flitting about from one place to another. Daniel 10:10–14 speaks of an angel who was delayed because of another spirit. So angels can't be more than one place at a time.

Angels were created to inhabit certain realms. Some are in heaven with God. Some are given special assignments over nations. For example, Michael is called the archangel, or special protector, of Israel (Dan. 12:1). Perhaps other angels are assigned to other countries to fulfill God's purpose within those borders.

Although angels are mostly invisible, at times they take on human form. Hebrews 13:2 says, "Do not neglect to show hospitality to strangers, for by this some have entertained angels without knowing it." Abraham and Sarah learned that lesson the awkward way when they entertained people they later found out were actual angels in disguise (Gen. 18:1–15).

Sometimes the appearance of angels can be downright frightening. Think about the Roman soldiers guarding the tomb of Jesus when the angel rolled the stone away. They were frozen in panic (Matt. 28:4). Or think about Gabriel's appearances to Mary, Elizabeth, and the shepherds. In each case, the angel's first words were, "Fear not."

Angels Minister to Believers

The writer of Hebrews gave us an ideal starting point in understanding the role of angels: "Are they not all ministering spirits, sent out to render service for the sake of those who will inherit salvation?" (1:14). We can think of angels as God's AAA service: always available to assist, on call day and night to render service to Christians who are in need. The Bible identifies four areas of service that angels provide for believers.

First, *God uses angels to sustain and encourage us.* Angels can provide for our physical needs, especially in times of stress. We see an example of this in Jesus's life. After forty days of fasting and testing in the wilderness, Jesus was in a vulnerable condition. Matthew 4:11 says, "Then the devil left Him; and behold, angels came and began to minister to Him." We shouldn't be surprised that angels do the same for us as well.

Second, *angels reveal God's will to us.* An angel revealed to Joseph that he was to take Mary as his wife (1:20–21). And an angel revealed to Philip a person who needed his help (Acts 8:26). A word of caution: any message we receive from an angel must align with God's Word. In 2 Corinthians 11:14, Paul warned that Satan can appear as an angel of light. Any angelic message that contradicts the Word of God comes from the devil.

Third, *angels protect us from physical and spiritual harm.* As startling as it may seem, one of Satan's chief strategies is

DO CHRISTIANS HAVE GUARDIAN ANGELS?

There is no passage in Scripture that explicitly states that every person has his or her own guardian angel. There are, however, a few passages, such as Psalm 91:11-12, Matthew 18:10, and Acts 12:13-15, that seem to support the idea of guardian angels.

However, as John Calvin pointed out in addressing this question, if there are legions of angels perpetually looking after our safety and well-being, it doesn't really matter whether there's one specific angel assigned to every person, does it?[1]

to cause your premature death. If you're not yet a Christian, he would love to kill you before you have an opportunity to trust in Christ. If you are a Christian, especially if you have an effective witness for God, he would love to kill you and extinguish that witness. Passages such as Psalm 91:11–12 suggest that angels keep him from doing it.

Even more amazing than the physical protection is the spiritual protection angels give us. Ephesians 6:12 says there is a spiritual war going on that we can't see, but we can feel it. The oppression, depression, and temptations we experience don't come out of nowhere: they're part of the demonic world that touches our lives. Daniel 10 offers a glimpse of that world. Daniel was feeling oppressed and discouraged, so he prayed to God. But for three weeks, no answer came. An angel finally appeared to Daniel and explained that he would have come sooner but was delayed by a demonic spirit.

There is an unseen but very real battle going on in the other world that affects us in this world.

Finally, *God uses angels to minister to us in death*. Revelation 14:13 says, "Blessed are the dead who die in the Lord." For Christians, death is a blessed experience because we don't have to face it alone. God sends His angels to usher our spirit into His presence. Look at the story of the rich man and Lazarus in Luke 16. According to verse 22, when Lazarus died, he "was carried away by the angels to Abraham's bosom." Angels will do the same for us as well. We will not face death alone.

Angels Fill Crucial Roles in God's Plan

The work of angels is not confined to believers alone. The Bible reveals at least three ways in which angels intervene in the lives of unbelievers. First, *they serve as ministers of God's goodness*. There was no sign that Hagar, the handmaid who gave birth to Ishmael, Abraham's first son, was a believer. Yet when Hagar and her unborn son were abandoned in the wilderness, an angel appeared to her and assured her that God would care for them both (Gen. 16:7–12).

Second, *angels serve as ministers of judgment against unbelievers*. Angels unleashed ten plagues on Egypt (Ps. 78:49). They slaughtered 185,000 Assyrian soldiers (2 Kings 19:35). And they struck down Herod and allowed his body to be devoured by worms (Acts 12:23). There's no reason to believe this morbid work of angels ended when the Scripture narrative did. The obituaries of unbelievers today list any number of causes of death: heart attack, cancer, car accident, and so forth. But sometimes—not always—the cause is an angel serving as a minister of judgment.

Third, *angels will serve as ministers of eternal death.*
According to Matthew 13:49–50, when unbelievers will be
thrown into the lake of fire after God's final judgment, angels will do the throwing. The last thing unbelievers will see
before being cast into hell will be the face of an angel.

The Bad—Satan and the Demons

In many respects, the transition from talking about angels
to talking about demons isn't much of a leap. Demons *are*
angels. They're just fallen ones. So if our angelic allies are
formidable—and they are—then by definition, so are our
demonic enemies.

As is the case with all warfare, the key to defeating demons
is intelligence. The more we know about our enemies' battle
strategies, the better prepared we can be to defend ourselves.[2]
But three difficult truths complicate our planning: demons
defy our expectations, attempt to lead believers astray, and
attempt to harm believers. So we need to understand the
influence demons can have over us.

Demons Defy Our Expectations

Contrary to popular Hollywood lore, demons generally
don't project themselves as monstrous, fire-spewing dragon-
snakes. Or as horned mini devils, for that matter. In fact,
demons probably would prefer that we not notice them at
all. Stealth makes their work easier. The key to their battle
plan is subtlety.

Have you ever felt an inexplicable weight of oppression
you just can't shake? Have you ever been in an argument that
turned hostile for no apparent reason? Have you ever had a

LUCIFER AND THE FALLEN ANGELS

Lucifer was an angel created by God. However, unlike other angels, Lucifer misused the free will God gave him. Ezekiel 28 and Isaiah 14 portray Lucifer as a proud, vain being who became overly impressed with his own beauty, intelligence, and power. Jealous of the honor and glory that belonged to God alone, he led a doomed rebellion of angels against the Creator.

Lucifer and his followers were banished from living in heaven, although Lucifer—who is now known as Satan—still has access to it. Satan's purpose now is to thwart God's work and destroy His people.

productive day suddenly derailed by a debilitating anxiety attack or faced a temptation that seemed custom-designed to entrap you? If you answered yes to any of these questions, then you've likely experienced demonic work in your life—just perhaps not in the way you expected.

Demons also defy our expectations in their attitude toward Jesus. We would certainly expect them to oppose Jesus's work on earth, and they did. They viewed His arrival as an invasion of their territory. Jesus came to reclaim this world from the grip of Satan and deliver it back to God. When He died on the cross, Jesus broke Satan's stranglehold. The nature of Jesus's mission explains why demons were more active in the world during His lifetime than at any other time in human history. They worked overtime to stop His plan from being fulfilled.

Yet demons were also staunch believers in Jesus. They couldn't help but be. They were witnesses to everything He did. They saw His birth as clearly as Mary and Joseph did. They saw Him counter every temptation their leader threw His way. They saw His miracles. They saw His crucifixion. They saw His empty tomb.

The New Testament author James wrote his letter to a group of Jewish Christians who prided themselves on believing that God is one, a basic principle of Judaism. Look at how James punctured their misplaced spiritual pride: "You believe that God is one. You do well; the demons also believe, and shudder" (James 2:19). In Luke 8:28, a man under the control of demons acknowledged Jesus as the Son of the Most High God.

Demons never put saving faith in Christ, but they did believe Jesus was who He claimed to be. And that belief gave them some dangerous insight into the nature of human beliefs.

Demons Attempt to Lead Unbelievers Astray

The twisted irony is that even though demons recognize the truth about Jesus, their goal is to lead people as far from the truth as possible. Their work in the lives of unbelievers is to exploit and redirect the innate human desire to know God and worship something greater than ourselves. Their first course of action is to lure people away from the true God using false gods.

The Old Testament contains only two references to demons, and both involve false gods. In Deuteronomy 32:17, Moses wrote, "They sacrificed to demons who were not God, to gods whom they have not known, new gods who came lately, whom your fathers did not dread." Moses was talking about the Canaanite gods the Israelites started worshiping after they entered the promised land. The Israelites thought they were making sacrifices to false gods such as Baal, Molech, and the like. As it turns out, they were actually sacrificing to demons.

Thousands of years later, the ruse continues. Behind every false god in the world today is a very real demonic power. Do you think it's any coincidence that two of the fastest-growing

UP CLOSE AND PERSONAL WITH DEMONS

Luke 8 tells of Jesus's confrontation with demons who were tormenting a man in the country of the Gerasenes. From this encounter, we discover four things about demons:

1. Demons have *intellect*. They immediately recognized Jesus as the Son of the Most High God.
2. Demons have *emotions*. They were afraid of being cast into the abyss.
3. Demons have a *will*. They offered Jesus an alternative solution: to be cast into a herd of swine. When Jesus agreed, they submitted themselves to the will of God and entered the swine.
4. Demons have *names*. The chief demon identified himself as Legion, a military term for a group of six thousand soldiers.

As believers in Jesus Christ, we need not fear demons, but we do need to understand them.

false religions in the world today, Islam and Mormonism, both have roots in angelic revelation? In AD 610, Muhammad claimed that the angel Gabriel gave him the revelation that became the Qur'an. In 1827, Joseph Smith claimed that the angel Moroni showed him where certain golden plates were buried. Smith said he used those plates to publish the Book of Mormon.

It's very likely that Muhammad and Joseph Smith *did* receive revelations from angels. But they weren't God's angels; they were Satan's. The Bible tells us that Satan can appear as an angel of light, a messenger. That's why we must remain steadfast in our beliefs. Any religion that denies that salvation is exclusively through the Lord Jesus Christ is a false, demonic religion being used by evil forces to lure people away from the true God.

An even more insidious way that demons lead unbelievers astray is by subtly tweaking aspects of the true gospel. For example, in the first-century Galatian church, a group known as the Judaizers taught that a person had to trust Christ for salvation—and also keep the Old Testament law through circumcision and dietary restrictions. Doing all those things would lead to eternal life, they said.

They lied. Theirs was a false gospel that denied the sufficiency of Christ's death and resurrection. It added to the simple gospel message that salvation is by faith in Christ alone. If you think you have to trust in Christ plus do anything else for your salvation, then you're being deceived by demons. That's why John warned, "Beloved, do not believe every spirit, but test the spirits to see whether they are from God, because many false prophets have gone out into the world" (1 John 4:1).

Demons Attempt to Harm Believers

Of course, demons aren't content merely to focus on unbelievers. Satan, their master, has a plan for believers as well—one his demons are only too happy to carry out. If Satan can't rob your soul for all eternity, then he wants to destroy every good thing in your life. Let's look at five methods demons use to accomplish his plan.

First, *demons can work through nature.* In Ephesians 2:2, Satan is called "the prince of the power of the air." God has given him and his demons limited authority over the natural elements in this world, such as wind, rain, hurricanes, and tornadoes. They can use the forces of nature to bring discouragement and loss into our lives, as they did with Job in the Old Testament.

Second, *demons can work through physical illness.* In 2 Corinthians 12:7, Paul explained that his "thorn in the flesh"—which was likely some physical ailment—was "a messenger of Satan." But he went on to say that God was using it for a good purpose, so that Paul wouldn't become proud and so that the power of Christ would dwell in his life. So even though a demon brought his ailment, ultimately it was under God's control.

Third, *demons can work through mental illness.* Our thoughts and emotions are more than a series of chemical and electrical impulses. External spiritual sources can affect them as well. In Philippians 4:6–7, Paul identified prayer as a positive spiritual exercise we can engage in to relieve anxiety. And if there's a positive spiritual force that can affect our thinking and emotions, then doesn't it stand to reason there are also negative spiritual forces that can impact them?

Now, let me be clear: it's a mistake to say all mental illness is a result of demonic activity. I remember asking a Christian psychiatrist, "How do you account for what the Bible calls demonic activity in relation to modern medical diagnoses of mental illness? Do you believe demons are responsible for these kinds of mental disorders?" The psychiatrist asked me a very good question in return. He said, "If all mental illnesses were the result of demonic activity, then why do the symptoms of mental disorders disappear almost completely with the right medical treatment?" The fact is, it's possible for chemical reactions and electrical impulses in the brain not to respond as they should. And many times those things should be treated with medicine.

Fourth, *demons can work through suicide*. We see this dark strategy in Mark 9, where a boy controlled by a demon is said to have thrown himself into fire and water. Demons are able to override our natural instinct for self-preservation and cause us to want to destroy our lives.

In John 8:44, Jesus refers to Satan as a liar and a murderer. Satan knows that when we get discouraged, we're vulnerable to his lies. That's when one of his demons starts whispering, "Your situation is hopeless; there's no way out of this." Or, "Nobody cares about you; nobody loves you." Or, "You've become a burden to your loved ones; it would be better for everyone if you just ended your life." Those thoughts don't come from God. They come from our enemy.

Fifth, *demons can work through people*. Yad Vashem, the World Holocaust Remembrance Center in Jerusalem, offers a solemn reminder of this. Every time I've taken a group there, we've emerged from it speechless at the horror of the

WHERE IS SATAN RIGHT NOW?

Even though Satan's work is being done on earth, he's not necessarily the one doing it. According to Revelation 12, Satan is in heaven, where he levels constant accusations against believers. He is doing everything he can to get God to change the deal He made with us for eternal life. Satan points at our sins and says, "Look at what she's doing. How can she call herself a Christian?" Or, "Why would You want to spend eternity with him? Let me have him."

The good news is that every time Satan levels an accusation against Christians, Jesus acts as our Advocate (1 John 2:1). Seated at the right hand of God the Father, He counters Satan's charges by reminding His Father of the price He, Jesus, paid for our sins.

torture and murder the Nazis inflicted on the Jewish people. When you see those horrific images, you wonder, *How could one human being do that to another human being?* The answer is in the question itself. It's not one human being doing it; it's demonic influence.

Of course, demonic work through other people rarely goes to such extremes. Remember, subtlety is the demons' specialty. Demons are content simply to deceive you into disobeying God. Their deception may involve an old flame who suddenly reappears during a rocky time in your marriage, tempting you to do something immoral. Or demons may try to discourage you by using someone who's willing to write a hateful email or social media post. They want you to feel so depressed and insecure when you read it that you can't focus on anything else. Their goal is to keep you from accomplishing God's purpose in your life.

Can Christians Be Demon-Possessed?

This strategy of demons using people, including believers, to accomplish their work raises an important question: Can Christians be demon-possessed? In answering it, we need to understand that the Greek word translated as "possessed" in passages such as Luke 8 actually means "demonized," or under the influence of demons.

"Demon-possessed" is not an accurate term for Christians. To *possess* something means to own it. Christians can't be owned by demons. Look again at Paul's words in Ephesians 1:13: "Having also believed, you were sealed in Him with the Holy Spirit of promise." The moment you trust in Christ as your Savior, you receive not only the forgiveness of your sins but also the sealing by the Holy Spirit. The Holy Spirit is God's stamp of ownership on your life. And God doesn't believe in joint ownership. He doesn't share His possessions with anyone. If God owns something, no one else can own it. That means it's impossible for believers to be possessed by demons.

The same is not true for unbelievers. In fact, every person who is not sealed by the Holy Spirit is possessed by Satan and his demons. Yes, you read that right. We're not born into this world as free agents. We're born into Satan's kingdom, and he has ownership of every person in it. It's only through Christ that we're rescued from the kingdom of darkness and placed into the kingdom of light (Col. 1:13).

That's not to suggest that every unbeliever has his head spin around like Linda Blair in *The Exorcist*. But it does mean that demons are free to do whatever they want with unbelievers.

Can Christians Be Controlled by Demons?

In Matthew 16, Jesus laid out for His disciples His plan of going to Jerusalem, dying, and being raised on the third day. And Peter, being Peter, said something to the effect of, "Lord, You don't need to suffer on the cross and die! There's a better way."

Jesus's response came fast and furious in verse 23: "He turned and said to Peter, 'Get behind Me, Satan! You are a stumbling block to Me; for you are not setting your mind on God's interests, but man's.'" Peter was allowing himself to be controlled by Satan through his words.

Acts 4–5 offers a more tragic example of demonic control of believers. In the church of Jerusalem, Barnabas sold a piece of property and gave all the proceeds to the church. People applauded his generosity. Seeing the praise and attention Barnabas received, a married couple named Ananias and Sapphira announced that they, too, were going to sell a piece of property and give every bit of the proceeds to the church. But they didn't follow through on their promise. They withheld a portion of the money for themselves.

"Peter said, 'Ananias, why has Satan filled your heart to lie to the Holy Spirit and to keep back some of the price of the land?'" (Acts 5:3). The Holy Spirit then struck Ananias dead in front of the whole church. Ananias was a believer. He had been baptized with the Holy Spirit, but he was being controlled by Satan. How do you explain that?

As we discovered in our examination of God the Holy Spirit, there's a difference between being baptized by the

Holy Spirit and being filled by the Holy Spirit. The baptism with the Holy Spirit is a one-time act of God by which, at the moment of our salvation, the Holy Spirit joins us to Jesus Christ, the head, and to all the other members of the body. Every true Christian has been baptized by the Holy Spirit. But not every Christian has been filled with the Holy Spirit.

In Ephesians 5:18, Paul said, "Be filled with the Spirit." That word translated as "filled" means "controlled." The filling of the Holy Spirit is the control of the Holy Spirit over our lives. The moment you become a Christian, you have all of the Holy Spirit. But does the Holy Spirit have all of you?

That's the key question when it comes to demonic influence. Any part of your life that's not being controlled by the Holy Spirit is open to being controlled by demons. We're not a spiritual vacuum. We may tell ourselves, *I'll hold off on committing this part of my life to God. I'll retain control over my dating life, my finances, and my career, and I'll give God the rest.* But it doesn't work that way. Any part of your life that is not under the control of the Holy Spirit is open to demonic influence.

The Upshot—A Strategy for Spiritual Victory

Now that we have intelligence dossiers on our allies and adversaries in the unseen spiritual war raging all around us, what do we do with this information? How can we build battle strategies that maximize the advantages God gives us through His angels? How can we minimize the destructive power of demons in our lives?

134

Let's start with the counteroffensive. The most effective way to neutralize demonic forces in our lives is to limit their staging area. We do that by placing every part of our lives under the Holy Spirit's control. If we insist on holding back anything—our finances, for example—from the Spirit's control, then we're putting a key battleground in play. We're handing demons the power to plant doubts in our minds about our long-term financial security. To make us believe we need a savings cushion before we embark on an overseas mission opportunity or convince us that our tithes are a discretionary budget item. More to the point, we're giving demons the opportunity to establish a foothold in our lives.

Our strategy is clear. We must resist the urge to hold back certain areas of our lives. We must be willing to give the Holy Spirit all of us. And it's a decision we must make every day—multiple times a day, if necessary. Because the temptation to grab the wheel never goes away. Demons looking for a way into our lives will try to convince us that we're capable of handling our own finances or resisting sexual temptation or controlling our anxiety without the Spirit's help.

So *diligence* is our watchword. We must continually examine our motives, aims, and priorities to make sure that every bit of our lives remains under the control of the Holy Spirit. That's how we emerge victorious from a cosmic battle.

As for maximizing the advantages God gives us through His angels, our best strategy is boldness. If Satan can make us feel alone, unsupported, and overwhelmed by his onslaught, he can neutralize us before the battle even begins. He can rob us of our power by causing us to doubt that we have it. Of course, the reality is quite different.

A Proper Perspective of the Spiritual Battlefield

Let's wrap up our examination of the fifth core belief of Christian theology by looking at an obscure but revealing story from 2 Kings 6. Elisha the prophet and his servant were living in the city of Dothan when they were surrounded by an army of mounted soldiers sent by the king of Aram. The king was intent on destroying Elisha, and it looked as though he was going to succeed. Escape was impossible, considering the size of the force arrayed against the prophet and his servant. Death seemed certain.

Elisha's servant panicked, which was understandable. Elisha didn't, which wasn't. The servant cried out to the prophet, "Alas, my master! What shall we do?" (v. 15).

In Elisha's next two sentences, we find all the truth and inspiration we need to fight every spiritual battle we will ever face. First, Elisha said to his servant, "Do not fear, for those who are with us are more than those who are with them" (v. 16). That's true of angels, as Elisha's servant was about to discover. But we don't need angels to tilt the balance in our fight against Satan and his demons. God alone is infinitely greater than all the forces of evil. If we belong to Him completely, we will emerge victorious because of His overwhelming superiority.

Second, Elisha prayed, "O Lord, I pray, open his eyes that he may see" (v. 17). Here's what happened next: "And the Lord opened the servant's eyes and he saw; and behold, the mountain was full of horses and chariots of fire all around Elisha." The servant's fears vanished when he saw all the angels ready to help him.

Sometimes all we need to be victorious in our battle against Satan and his forces is a proper perspective of the battlefield.

6

HUMANITY AND SIN

Did you know that the word *naughty* once meant to have nothing—or naught? ("He used to be wealthy, but reckless spending left him *naughty*.")

Or that the word *awful* once meant to be worthy of awe? ("Helen of Troy possessed an *awful* beauty.")

Or that the word *nice* once meant unintelligent or ignorant? ("I wouldn't trust him to make the right decision—he's too *nice*.")

Words change with the culture. In some cases, their meanings can turn 180 degrees. A term that once had a positive connotation can become negative. A compliment can become an insult. With that quirk of etymology in mind, let's consider the word *human*.

For a brief, shining moment, to be human was to look forward to an unimaginably bright future, filled with God's continuous blessings. From Genesis 1:26 to Genesis 2:25, to be human was to embody the pinnacle of God's creative work. To be human was to reflect God's image. To be human was to be animated by the breath of the Holy Spirit. To be human was to enjoy the privilege of God's company. To be human was to be entrusted with the care and maintenance of God's handiwork. To be human was to glimpse the full potential of God's plan for creation.

To say, "I'm human," was the loftiest possible form of self-affirmation, a reminder of all that God, in His creative genius and limitless generosity, had laid out before us.

Then came Genesis 3.

After the fall of Adam and Eve in the garden of Eden, the idea of being human took on new shades of meaning. Its luster dimmed. Today, we often use the word *human* as a catch-all defense for our worst instincts:

- "I should have resisted when she invited me back to her place, but I'm only human."
- "I'm sorry I went off on you like that. My human nature just got the better of me."
- "Don't try to put me on a pedestal. I'm human just like everyone else."

In his poem "An Essay on Criticism," Alexander Pope captured the reality of our dimmed luster in four simple words: "To err is human."[1]

In our study of the sixth core belief of Christianity, we will explore the sudden shift in what it means to be human. To fully understand this shift, we will look at God's original plan for humanity. Then we'll look at the far-reaching impact of our rejection of His plan. Finally—and thankfully—we will look at God's refusal to allow our sin to have the last word.

The Way We Were

Quaker poet John Greenleaf Whittier probably wasn't thinking of the first two chapters of Genesis when he wrote his 1856 poem "Maud Muller." But his words capture the lost possibilities of God's original creation all the same: "For of all sad words of tongue or pen, the saddest are these: 'It might have been!'"[2] In Genesis 1–2, we get a glimpse of what might have been. And the realization is heartbreaking.

In the first two chapters of Genesis, we see God's creation firing on all cylinders. The entire world probably still had that new-universe smell. We get a brief glimpse of all created beings—especially humans—embracing and fulfilling their God-given purpose.

The psalmists recognized the potential of nature to fulfill God's purposes:

- "O LORD, our Lord, how majestic is Your name in all the earth, who have displayed Your splendor above the heavens!" (8:1).
- "The heavens are telling of the glory of God; and their expanse is declaring the work of His hands" (19:1).
- "The heavens will praise Your wonders, O LORD; Your faithfulness also in the assembly of the holy ones" (89:5).

God created everything for His glory—so that His perfections would be recognized, acknowledged, and celebrated. The purpose of our existence is to bring glory and honor to Him. You may be wondering, "If God wanted people to praise Him all the time, why didn't He delete all our other functions except the worship app? Why didn't He create us so that all we want to do is worship Him?" It seems like a simple enough fix. Think of it this way: If you had the inclination and the know-how, you could program an artificial intelligence robot to bow down to you every hour, on the hour. You could have your invention sing songs of praise written especially for you. You could make it tell you how great you are every time you walk into a room.

But what purpose would that serve? There's nothing genuine or heartfelt about a programmed response. For real, meaningful worship to take place, there must be a choice—an option *not* to worship. For real, meaningful obedience to occur, there must be an option *not* to obey.

Likewise, God desires a genuine personal relationship with us. But in order for a relationship to be genuine, there must be an option to walk away from it. Otherwise, the relationship would be a coerced arrangement.

In other words, there must be free will.

Glorifying God in the way He intends us to involves every aspect of our being. We glorify Him with our minds by thinking of Him. We glorify Him with our hearts by loving Him. We glorify Him with our wills by choosing to obey Him.

As long as Adam and Eve chose to obey, the garden of Eden was a paradise—that is, a paradise for two. But in God's instructions to the man and woman, we find hints of His bigger plan. In Genesis 1:28, He said to Adam and Eve,

"Be fruitful and multiply, and fill the earth, and subdue it." A chapter later, in the extended account of humanity's creation, we find the interconnectedness between humans and the earth. God held back the rain and the resulting vegetation until His human creation was in place to cultivate it. God put the systems in place for the earth to bloom and provide a home and sustenance for His people (2:5–15).

But the harvest would require the participation of humans. God's blessings were ready to be enjoyed, but we had to get our hands dirty to bring them forth. God's original plan for men and women was for us to work in harmony with Him to maximize the potential of His creation. He surrounded us with a perfect ecosystem—not for us to enjoy as spectators but for us to cultivate. He intended for us to be equal parts producers and consumers.

The oneness of the natural world in God's original plan is remarkable. As the animals presented themselves to Adam to be named, there was no hint of predator or prey. Plants, trees, and rivers provided nourishment for all creatures. Humans performed the necessary tasks to ensure they would continue to provide.

All of nature was in perfect harmony, and humans enjoyed the vital role of working with God to maintain that harmony—and expand the borders of paradise.

As mentioned earlier, the garden of Eden was a paradise for two. And in God's original plan, as Adam and Eve had children, that paradise would have to be expanded. God's command to "subdue" the earth in Genesis 1:28 suggests that the expansion would require work on our part. But it was work with guaranteed results. Again, God's creative blessings were there, beyond the garden, waiting to be cultivated.

Our continuing efforts to subdue the earth, as needed, would directly benefit us. We would literally be able to taste the fruits of our labor. In turn, the enjoyment and satisfaction we derived from cultivating God's creation would lead to a greater appreciation of and love for our Creator. Our ever-deepening relationship with Him would satisfy our souls just as His physical handiwork satisfied our bodies. To top it off, we could look forward to His visits in the cool of the day (3:8).

For a time, we knew what it was to live in paradise.

The Way It Ended

Anyone who's ever read a comic book or watched a super-hero movie knows that with much power comes much responsibility. And with apologies to the Man of Steel and Spider-Man, the greatest human power of all is free will. Our power comes not from the planet Krypton or a radioactive spider bite but from God Himself. He gave us the ability to defy Him, to make decisions apart from what He would have us choose.

Of course, with great responsibility comes great consequences. Unfortunately, in the case of Adam and Eve—and their descendants—the magnitude of the consequences didn't sink in until it was too late.

A Fateful Decision

As I mentioned earlier, the blessings of God's perfect plan were contingent on our obedience. As long as we chose to follow God's commands, we could enjoy Eden forever. So to put in context what happened next, we need to review

WHY DID GOD PLANT THE FORBIDDEN TREE IN THE GARDEN?

The Bible doesn't spell out God's reasons for planting the tree of the knowledge of good and evil—the tree from which He forbade Adam and Eve to eat—in the garden of Eden. But this tree gave Adam and Eve an opportunity to honor God in a meaningful way.

Imagine you're walking on a beach with your spouse. Up ahead you see a good-looking person, dressed to show off—a potential object of lust for your spouse. As other couples pass by, you notice various spouses reacting to the person, some obviously, some less so. As you approach, your spouse glances at the would-be temptation and then turns his or her full attention to you, not giving the person a second look or thought.

By resisting temptation, your spouse honored you and your relationship in a way that wouldn't have been possible otherwise. The same goes for the tree in the garden. Every time Adam and Eve walked past it and chose not to eat from it, they honored God.

all the things God said that Adam and Eve could *not* do in the garden. Compiled from Genesis 1–3, the complete list is as follows:

1. *Do not eat the fruit from the tree of the knowledge of good and evil.*

Yes, that's the whole list. Just one restriction.

Every tree, every luscious fruit in the garden of Eden, was available to Adam and Eve—except one. Let's do the math. How many trees do you imagine were in God's original creation? One hundred? One thousand? Ten thousand? Whatever the number, the ratio of God's blessings to His restrictions was astronomical. Maybe 100 to 1. Or 1,000 to 1. Or even 10,000 to 1.

Yet Satan, in the guise of a serpent, managed to turn those ratios to his favor using one of the greatest illusions of all time. You may have seen the famous magician David Copperfield convince audiences that he can fly and make the Statue of Liberty disappear by directing their attention where he wants it to go and distracting them from what he doesn't want them to see. That's exactly what Satan did in Genesis 3. He managed to blind Eve to God's immeasurable blessings by getting her to fixate on God's lone restriction. He convinced her that the Lord's one prohibition canceled out His astonishing generosity. "The one thing you can't have is the only thing that will make you truly happy" was his deceitful message to her. "God doesn't want you to eat it, because He's afraid you'll become like Him if you do. And He won't be able to push you around anymore."

Satan's strategy worked so well with Eve that he continues to use variations of it today:

- "God never lets you do any fun stuff, does He?"
- "Being made in the image of God means you can make your own decisions and find your own meaning in life."
- "Does God really need to micromanage every aspect of your life? Is He that insecure?"

For just a moment, Eve was blinded to the blessings of God that surrounded her. She forgot that great responsibility comes with great power. And for the first time, she used her free will to choose to disobey God.

"When the woman saw that the tree was good for food, and that it was a delight to the eyes, and that the tree was desirable to make one wise, she took from its fruit and ate; and she gave also to her husband with her, and he ate" (Gen. 3:6). In a single moment, Adam and Eve changed their world forever. They pawned the perfection of God's creation for a lie of Satan.

In this heartbreaking passage, we see a subtle but very real difference between Eve's actions and Adam's actions. The apostle Paul elaborated on this difference. In his first letter to Timothy, Paul wrote, "It was not Adam who was deceived, but the woman being deceived, fell into transgression" (2:14).

Compare that to Paul's words to the believers in Rome: "Through one man sin entered into the world, and death through sin, and so death spread to all men, because all sinned" (Rom. 5:12). Eve was certainly guilty of disobeying God, but her disobedience stemmed from being deceived by the serpent. On the other hand, Adam deliberately defied the Creator's clear command. That explains why the condemnation of the entire human race is traced to Adam and not Eve.

Adam was patient zero for the sin virus. According to Paul, Adam's single act of disobedience allowed sin to spread to the entire human race. With only one exception, every descendant of Adam and Eve has been infected with sin. (We will examine that one exception in our study of the core belief of salvation.) As a result, every day of our lives we exhibit the same symptoms of infection. We show a marked defiance toward God and His commands. We don't recognize His wisdom or admit that it's best for us. We're determined to pursue our own desires, come what may. And we deceive ourselves into believing that we're basically good people.

Scripture offers no shortage of dire warnings about this infection of sin:

- "The LORD saw that the wickedness of man was great on the earth, and that every intent of the thoughts of his heart was only evil continually" (Gen. 6:5).
- "They are corrupt, they have committed abominable deeds; there is no one who does good. . . . They have all turned aside, together they have become corrupt; there is no one who does good, not even one" (Ps. 14:1, 3).
- "The heart is more deceitful than all else and is desperately sick; who can understand it?" (Jer. 17:9).

The sin that infects us is malignant; it leads to eternal death, whether we acknowledge it or not. The only diagnosis that matters comes from the only one who can see the full scope of our condition. The only one who truly understands what our sin has done is our holy God.

A Holy God

God is holy. That's important to remember. It's so important, in fact, that there are seraphim, angelic beings, in heaven who announce God's holiness continuously, according to the prophet Isaiah. In his vision, Isaiah saw the Lord, seated on His throne in heaven, surrounded by seraphim who called out, "Holy, Holy, Holy is the LORD of hosts" (Isa. 6:3).

Many people mistakenly assume that holiness is a benign concept, similar to goodness or morality. They think the seraphim's heavenly announcement is the equivalent of saying, "God is a good guy who stands for truth and justice."

But holiness goes far beyond goodness or morality. God's holiness has profound implications for us sin-infected descendants of Adam. The Hebrew word translated as "holy" comes from a term that means "to cut" or "to separate." God is separate from everything and everyone else in creation. In other words, He is "a cut above."

God's holiness means He is separate from sin. Such a concept was novel in the ancient world. Practitioners of false religions imagined their gods reveling in evil and immorality. But not so with the God of Abraham, Isaac, and Jacob. The prophet Habakkuk addressed the Lord this way: "Your eyes are too pure to approve evil, and You can not look on wickedness with favor" (1:13).

For clues as to how God's holiness affects us, take a look at how Isaiah reacted after he got just a fleeting glimpse of that holiness. He said, "Woe is me, for I am ruined! Because I am a man of unclean lips, and I live among a people of unclean lips; for my eyes have seen the King, the LORD of hosts" (6:5). The venerable prophet came unglued as he realized what God's holiness meant for him—and for the rest of God's people—forever.

The clearer God's holiness comes into focus, the clearer we see our own sinfulness and the reason He sets Himself apart from us. Understanding God's holiness gives us a sense of the distance our sin has created between us and Him.

147

A Vast Chasm

The prophet Isaiah certainly recognized that distance. He said, "Behold, the Lord's hand is not so short that it cannot save; nor is His ear so dull that it cannot hear. But your iniquities have made a separation between you and your God, and your sins have hidden His face from you so that He does not hear" (59:1–2).

We have no defense against this charge. The responsibility for the distance between us and God lies solely with us. God did nothing to us but provide for our every need, share His amazing creation with us, entrust us with a solemn responsibility, and show us how to find our deepest fulfillment by obeying Him. He has stayed absolutely true to His nature and unquestionably faithful to His promises.

The distance between us and God was created by Adam's and Eve's decisions to disobey in the garden—and by the similar decisions made every day by every one of their descendants (again, with one exception). As the old saying goes, "If you feel distant from God, guess which one of you moved?"

Of course, that doesn't stop us from trying to shift the blame—or at least trying to shift the focus. Since God is blameless, the only place we can point our finger is at one another. So we rationalize and make strategic comparisons designed to show ourselves in the best possible light. We use faulty standards to measure our goodness. We invoke the names of history's most notorious villains to show that, relatively speaking, we're not as bad as other people are.

In terms of distance from God, we may not be as near to Him as, say, Peter, Paul, Mary the mother of Jesus, and other heroes of the faith were. But we're certainly closer to Him than Adolf Hitler, Joseph Stalin, and the Christian-persecuting Roman emperor Nero were. And that has to count for something—or so we think.

The problem is, we underestimate the distance that our sin put between us and God.

To put it in terms we can picture, imagine that the chasm between us and God is the size of the Grand Canyon. God is on the North Rim of the canyon; we're on the South Rim. With no help from God, each of our lives would be like taking a running leap from the South Rim. Hitler and his ilk would stumble on takeoff, of course, and drop like stones. Most of us would surpass them by a good six or seven feet. The very best of us—the most morally upright people who ever lived—might get as far as twelve feet out from takeoff. But what does that matter when the distance between the North and South Rims is more than twenty miles?

With this Grand Canyon analogy in mind, the words of the apostle Paul in Romans 3:23 take on a new dimension: "All have sinned and fall short of the glory of God." The glory of God—the evidence of His perfections—is the very thing we were created to acknowledge and celebrate. The glory of God is the only thing in which we can find ultimate meaning and purpose. Yet due to the lethal combination of our sin and God's holiness, the glory of God is immeasurably beyond our reach.

We are powerless to close the distance between us and God. Unless we acknowledge that truth, the distance can never be closed. We can't bring God closer by being the best possible version of ourselves. We can't earn His favor through good works. We can't jump the gap, even with a good tailwind.

Our only hope for bridging the chasm between our sinfulness and God's holiness is for God to take the initiative and reach across to us. The bridge must start from His side.

The Way Back

You may have noticed that the Alexander Pope quote earlier in this chapter—"To err is human"—was incomplete. To put this sixth core belief of Christianity in context, to understand how humanity's sin and God's holiness can ever be reconciled, we need to finish the poet's thought:

"To err is human; to forgive, divine."[3]

Just as God's holiness can never be abated, neither can His love. The impossibly wide chasm between us and God that we created because of our sin is no match for God's love. Our way back to God begins with understanding what it cost God to redeem us and understanding that our battle against sin never ends.

A Plan of Redemption

To understand God's plan of redemption, we need to go back to the beginning, to Adam and Eve in the garden. A series of tragic "firsts" occurred in the wake of their decision to disobey God. Genesis 3:7 says, "The eyes of both of them were opened, and they knew that they were naked; and they sewed fig leaves together and made themselves loin coverings."

For the first time ever, humans experienced guilt. The rawness of the emotion caused Adam and Eve to feel exposed. Both had been naked since creation—unashamedly so, because they had nothing to hide. Yet after they sinned, Adam and Eve suddenly felt the need for a covering. Guilt provokes

LIKE FATHER, LIKE SON

In Romans 5:8, Paul said, "God demonstrates His own love toward us, in that while we were yet sinners, Christ died for us." However, even before He died for us, Jesus gave us tangible evidence of God's love for sinners.

Jesus spent so much time with despised members of Jewish society that the religious leaders of the day referred to Him as "a friend of tax collectors and sinners" (Matt. 11:19). They thought they were leveling a devastating criticism. They didn't realize Jesus would embrace the title.

Jesus was a friend of sinners. He cared about their well-being. He showed them a different way. And when they crucified Him, He said, "Father, forgive them" (Luke 23:34). Jesus loved sinners because God loves sinners. And our redemption begins with that amazing truth.

that same reaction in us even today. Instead of admitting our mistakes, our natural instinct is to try to cover them up and hope no one notices. This is part of the sin nature we inherited from Adam and Eve. The first couple tried to cover their sin using the materials they had on hand to fashion garments for themselves.

Meanwhile, God came looking for them "in the cool of the day" (v. 8), as was His custom. And for the first time, Adam and Eve dreaded God's presence. They became acutely aware of His holiness and realized their feeble efforts to cover themselves could not withstand His scrutiny.

As the awful weight of what they had done settled on them, Adam and Eve were able to receive God's first provision for their sin: "The LORD God made garments of skin for Adam and his wife, and clothed them" (v. 21). This is the first death recorded in Scripture. It's also the first sacrifice. It's the first reveal of the payment necessary for sin—and the first foreshadowing of the once-and-for-all sacrifice to come.

The skin for their coverings came from an animal God had created—a living creature He had to kill because of their sin. For the first time ever, something innocent died to cover the sins of someone guilty. And God provided the sacrificial animal.

Animal sacrifices, along with grain offerings, multiplied exponentially under the law of Moses. The never-ending need for offerings and sacrifices served as a perpetual reminder of the people's sins. These sacrifices didn't actually remove sins. Instead, they underscored people's need for forgiveness. They also foreshadowed the coming final sacrifice of Jesus Christ. The climax of Israel's annual cycle of offerings and sacrifices took place on the Day of Atonement, which is described in detail in Leviticus 16.

God wanted His people to understand that something innocent had to die to atone for those who are guilty. Even so, the covering of sins these animals provided was limited. These animals were simply object lessons that pointed to the ultimate sacrifice, Jesus Christ, whom God Himself would provide to atone for the sins of the world. Like the animal sacrifices, Jesus Christ was "without blemish" (Ezek. 43:22). But that's where the similarity stops.

- The Old Testament sacrifice system was perpetual. The offerings and sacrifices had to be made continually. But Jesus Christ was offered once, through His crucifixion.

- The Old Testament sacrifices were made by sinful priests who first had to atone for their own sins. Christ was the perfect, sinless High Priest who had no sin of His own to atone for, so He could present Himself as the ultimate sacrifice for our sins.
- The Old Testament sacrifices provided temporary reconciliation with God. Christ's sacrifice offered eternal redemption for those who believe (Heb. 9:11–12).

The Old Testament sacrificial system was designed to remind God's people every day of their sin and their need for atonement. The fact that those sacrifices were never completed but had to be offered year after year created a longing for the once-and-for-all sin offering that only God Himself could make.

That sacrifice is the focus of the seventh core belief of Christianity. In the chapter that follows, we will examine why Jesus Christ alone is able to provide salvation. As we wrap up this chapter, let's consider the lingering problem of sin.

A Continuing Battle

Jesus's death on the cross removed the penalty of our sin and destroyed the power of sin over us once and for all. But it didn't eliminate the presence of sin from our lives. The ultimate war is won, yet many battles remain. A defeated enemy with nothing to lose is a dangerous opponent. And Satan knows that the tactic that worked in the garden of Eden is every bit as effective today.

In his encounter with Eve, the serpent contradicted God and lied about Him. But he knew he couldn't deceive Eve until he had her attention. To get her attention without scaring her away, the serpent had to be subtle. He had to tap in the point of a wedge that he could use to greater effect later. And he did it with four simple words: "Did God really say . . . ?"

Tactically, it's a brilliant strategy. With these four words, Satan is able to plant doubts without directly challenging God. That comes later. "Did God really say?" could be as innocuous as "Are you sure you heard Him correctly?" or "Are you sure that's what He meant?"

Today the strategy behind those four words can take any number of forms:

- "Jesus never actually claimed to be the Messiah. That was a title His disciples gave Him after He died to bolster their own ministries."
- "God loves you and wants you to be happy. If someone or something makes you truly happy, questions of right and wrong no longer apply."
- "Jesus said, 'Love your neighbor.' You can't love someone if you don't accept them for who they are."

The devil's goal is to create static in the transmission of God's Word to our hearts. He wants to make us doubt whether we understand it correctly. When we doubt what we're most sure of, we're vulnerable to temptation and susceptible to sin.

Instead of allowing our understanding of God's Word to be our Achilles' heel, we can make it our first line of defense against Satan. We do that by studying Scripture in a purposeful way, seeking answers to difficult questions and working to understand why we believe what we do. We do that by spending time in prayer, asking God to reveal more truths from His Word. We do that by talking with church leaders and mature believers, drawing from their wisdom on difficult topics. We do that by engaging with people who don't necessarily share our views of God and Scripture, trying to answer their questions and respond to their objections. We do that by finding accountability partners who will challenge us when they see things in our lives that need to be brought to our attention.

The Beating Heart in Believers

Let's close this chapter by looking at one of the starkest representations of human sin in all of literature. The narrator of Edgar Allan Poe's short story "The Tell-Tale Heart" believes he has gotten away with murder after killing an old man and hiding his body under the floorboards of the house. The only hitch in his plan is the sound he hears afterward, which he believes is the beating of the old man's heart.

The narrator goes to great lengths to convince the reader of his sanity, even as the beating gets louder. He maintains a pleasant, casual facade when the police come to investigate, though the ever-louder beating starts to unnerve him. Finally, he can take no more. The sound of the beating heart—a manifestation of the narrator's guilt—drives him to madness and confession.

In a much less dramatic sense, the Holy Spirit serves as the beating heart in the lives of believers. He makes us aware of our guilt—our sin—and compels us to confess. Not to drive us mad, as in Poe's story, but to restore our spiritual well-being and our relationship with God.

Sin ruined God's original plan for humanity. God, in His infinite mercy, provided a plan of redemption so that our sin would not have the last word. Satan would like nothing more than to tarnish that redemption by coaxing the redeemed back into sin. But God has equipped us with everything we need to counter Satan's efforts. Thanks to God, humanity and sin are no longer inextricably linked.

7

SALVATION

If you're in the mood to start an argument, especially among men of a certain age, all you have to do is say these words: "The best way to get to _____ is _____." You can fill in the blanks with the destination and directions of your choosing. It doesn't matter. What matters is that regardless of what you say—even if it involves giving directions to your own house—that man will have a better way. It may take you through three industrial parks, down two blind alleys, and across the practice green of a golf course, but he claims it will be better because it shaves seven and a half seconds off your travel time. And he'll be prepared to defend that claim tooth and nail.

Imagine what the reaction would be if you claimed to know the *only* way to get somewhere!

Yet that very claim of exclusivity lies at the center of the seventh core belief of Christianity: salvation. Remember that Jesus said, "I am the way, and the truth, and the life; no one comes to the Father but through Me" (John 14:6). Jesus was clear: He is the only way to heaven. He left no room for other ways, other truths, other religions, or other paths to eternal life.[1] That's why the biblical concept of salvation is perhaps the most controversial of the ten core beliefs of Christianity.

Understanding Exclusivity

From the start, exclusivity has marked God's interaction with His people. In Exodus 20, He said, "I am the LORD your God. . . . You shall have no other gods before Me" (vv. 2–3).

God doesn't keep an open mind to a multiplicity of ideas. He doesn't reward creative alternatives to His plans. Sin caused a devastating rift in our relationship with Him. As a result, God is specific and exacting in His demands of us.

Consider the instructions He gave to Noah in Genesis 6:14–16 for building the ark. The most expertly crafted seaworthy vessel would not have saved the human race from the flood if it had not been constructed from the exact materials, built to the exact size, and included the exact number of decks and doors God required.

Consider the instructions He gave Moses in Exodus 25–30 for building the tabernacle. This ornate structure for religious gatherings would not have been sufficient for Jewish worship if it did not include every detail God laid out, down to the intricate design of the priestly garments.

Consider the instructions He gave His people in Leviticus 16–27 for sacrifices and offerings. The most heartfelt sacrifice to God would not have been acceptable if it did not conform to the exact requirements God spelled out.

Cain, the first son of Adam and Eve, learned that lesson the hard way when he and his brother Abel presented their offerings to the Lord. Genesis 4:3–5 says, "Cain brought an offering to the LORD of the fruit of the ground. Abel, on his part also brought of the firstlings of his flock and of their fat portions. And the LORD had regard for Abel and for his offering; but for Cain and for his offering He had no regard. So Cain became very angry and his countenance fell."

Most people get so caught up in the aftermath of this story—the first murder, the first lie to God—that they overlook an important question: Why did God reject Cain's offering and accept Abel's?

The answer may lie in what's *not* in the text. Somewhere between the events of Genesis 4:2 and 4:3, God may have given Cain and Abel specific instructions regarding the kind of offering He desired. Perhaps Abel followed those instructions while Cain rejected them. If that's the case, God likely required from both brothers an animal sacrifice as a reminder of the seriousness of sin and the necessity of blood to cover that sin.

Abel may not have understood the reasons for God's command, but still he obeyed it. Cain, on the other hand, opted for a different approach. Perhaps he thought a beautifully displayed arrangement of fruit and grain on the altar would be more aesthetically pleasing than a bloody animal. But God wasn't interested in a more pleasing approach to sacrifice. He wanted His people to be acutely reminded that their sin was so great that the blood of an innocent animal was required to cover their guilt.

Two New Testament passages shed additional light on this incident. The writer of Hebrews said, "By faith Abel offered to God a better sacrifice than Cain, through which he obtained the testimony that he was righteous, God testifying about his gifts, and through faith, though he is dead, he still speaks" (11:4). Jude went even further. He identified Cain's act of disobedience as the genesis of every false religion in the world today. "Woe to them! For they have gone the way of Cain" (v. 11).

- "The way of Cain" refers to any attempt to approach God on our own terms rather than on God's terms.
- "The way of Cain" describes any religious system that attempts to earn God's favor through works rather than through complete reliance on God's grace.
- "The way of Cain" is any religious system that appeals to our pride rather than our desperate condition before God.
- "The way of Cain" emphasizes human goodness rather than human sinfulness.
- "The way of Cain" says there are many paths that lead to God rather than one path.
- "The way of Cain" leads to eternal death rather than eternal life: "There is a way which seems right to a man, but its end is the way of death" (Prov. 14:12).

The message that comes through loud and clear throughout Scripture is this: if you want to be in a right relationship with the one true God, whom you have alienated by your sin, then you must reconcile with Him on His terms, not yours. God is, by His very nature, exclusive.

Four Objections to the Exclusivity of Jesus Christ

Jesus's claim to be the only way to God and the only means of salvation for humanity provokes strong objections in our increasingly inclusive culture. If you've engaged in conversations about the exclusivity of Jesus's sacrifice, you'll likely recognize four of the most common objections.

Objection #1: Exclusivity Is Intolerant

The first objection goes like this: if you claim that Jesus is the only path to God, you're being intolerant. And in our culture, there is no greater offense. The word *tolerance* has undergone a radical transformation in recent years. A generation ago, tolerance meant a respect for people's right to believe whatever they want to believe. Being tolerant meant acknowledging that people have the right to be wrong or to believe a lie if they so choose.

Today, however, tolerance requires a much more substantial commitment. To be tolerant today, we must say that all beliefs are equally valid.

In terms of spiritual beliefs, that leaves us in an awkward position. All major religions answer the question, "What must a person do to be right with God?" And for many religions, the answer is, by nature, exclusive. Yet the modern concept of tolerance doesn't allow for exclusivity. So our culture has moved the question from the realm of objective truth, in which there is a correct answer, to the realm of subjective truth, in which everyone's opinion is equally valid. When Christians attempt to shift it back to the realm of objective truth, we're accused of being intolerant.

Yet *Webster's New World Dictionary* defines *tolerate* as "to recognize and respect others' beliefs and practices without sharing them; to bear or put up with someone or something not necessarily liked."[2] If you are truly tolerant, it means you are respectful of beliefs and behaviors with which you disagree. You can only be truly tolerant of something you disagree with. For example, I can be respectful of Muslims, recognizing their freedom to believe whatever they want to believe, without embracing Islam as an alternative pathway to God.

Tolerance involves a choice. You come to a judgment that what a person is saying or doing is wrong, but you nevertheless show that person respect and give him or her the right to be wrong.

Objection #2: How Can So Many People Be So Wrong?

The second objection goes like this: if Jesus is the only way to be saved, that means an overwhelming number of people are facing eternity in hell. Billions of people throughout history never trusted Christ as their Savior. Instead, they followed the path of Islam or Buddhism or Hinduism or some other religion. How can so many people be so wrong? That question has particular weight in Western culture, which accepts that the majority is usually right and the minority is usually wrong.

According to the Pew Research Center, roughly 31 percent of the world's population can be labeled "Christian."[3] The percentage of true followers of Christ is much smaller than that—a miniscule number, when you consider how many people have ever lived. How could such a small percentage of people know the only real path to salvation? How could so many sincere people be wrong?

To answer these questions, we must acknowledge two truths about ourselves. First, humans were born with an inclination to worship someone or something greater than ourselves. We are spiritual beings. Ecclesiastes 3:11 says God "set eternity" in our hearts. We sense there is something that transcends this life.

Second, human beings are incurably rebellious. One of the residual effects of the sin virus we all inherited from Adam and Eve is the propensity to reject the knowledge of the true God and instead follow our own hearts. The problem with that approach is made abundantly clear in Jeremiah 17:9: "The heart is more deceitful than all else and is desperately sick; who can understand it?" That's how it's possible for so many people to be so wrong.

Jesus crunched the numbers in Matthew 7:13–14: "Enter through the narrow gate; for the gate is wide and the way is broad that leads to destruction, and there are many who enter through it. For the gate is small and the way is narrow that leads to life, and there are few who find it." In other words, the highway that leads to hell is a wide road, and most people in the world are on it. The path that leads to heaven is narrow; few people find it. Jesus Himself predicted that most people will spend eternity in hell.

As sobering as that thought is, even more jarring is the idea that many of those on the path to hell are religious people. In verse 21, Jesus said, "Not everyone who says to Me, 'Lord, Lord,' will enter the kingdom of heaven, but he who does the will of My Father who is in heaven will enter.'"

The fact that most people miss the way to heaven doesn't negate the truth of exclusivity; it proves it, because Jesus predicted it. Isn't it logical to assume that Jesus is also right in His prescription of how to escape hell through faith in Him?

Objection #3: All Religions Are Basically the Same

The third objection goes like this: Jesus's claim of exclusivity doesn't make sense because all religions teach basically the same thing. At the heart of this objection is the notion that all world religions spring from people's sincere desire to seek God. People with this objection say that individual experiences and cultural realities cause people to pursue different paths. They say God cares only about the sincerity that fuels a person's journey to Him, not about the path that person chooses.

The Word of God sees it another way. According to Scripture, the fact that there are so many religions in the world is evidence not of the sincerity of human beings but of the sinfulness of human beings. In Romans 1:22–23, Paul said, "Professing to be wise, they became fools, and exchanged the glory of the incorruptible God for an image in the form of corruptible man and of birds and four-footed animals and crawling creatures." In other words, the people who created idols didn't really believe those images were God. Instead, those people rejected the truth of the real God and replaced it with gods of their own liking—ones that were more convenient or manageable. The same goes for every manmade religion. Its followers have rejected the truth of God and replaced it with a truth of their own creation.

That's one biblical explanation for the origin of world religions. A second explanation is even more alarming. In Psalm 106:36–37, the psalmist revealed that behind every false god is a demon. So when the people of Israel were making sacrifices to the pagan gods of other nations, they were actually sacrificing to demons.

That biblical truth doesn't change, even when a deity has billions of followers. Behind every other world religion—including Buddhism, Hinduism, and Islam—is a demon sent by Satan to deceive people and lead them away from the truth.

The way you deceive people is by mixing a lot of error with a little bit of truth. And that's how Satan works in world religions today. He provides just enough common ground to convince people there are no substantial differences between other religions and Christianity. He encourages us to relax the exclusivity that God demands.

Objection #4: It's Unfair for God to Send People to Hell

The fourth objection goes like this: it's unfair for God to send people to hell just because they haven't believed in Jesus. After all, not everyone has heard the gospel message—that Jesus Christ is the Son of God who died on the cross to pay the penalty for our sins, rose from the grave by the power of God, and now offers us forgiveness and eternal life. There are people who have never heard of Jesus. How can they be expected to believe?

Acts 17:26 seems to bolster the objection: "[God] made from one man every nation of mankind to live on all the face of the earth, having determined their appointed times and the boundaries of their habitation." This verse suggests that God determines where we live. He decides whether we're born in America or India or Africa. So if God has placed people in an area where the gospel has not been preached, how can He be justified in sentencing them to hell because they never believed in Jesus?

The two problems with this objection are that it overestimates people's ignorance of God and underestimates people's ability to recognize Him. One of the bedrock principles of Scripture is that God will reveal Himself to those who want to know Him. In fact, He already has.

In Romans 1:18–20, Paul said anyone can look into the heavens—or any aspect of creation—and realize it didn't happen by accident. Anyone can look at nature and know there is a power greater than him- or herself. You don't have to read a Bible to know there is a God. Theologically speaking, this is known as general revelation. Everyone who has ever been born has this knowledge of God.

General revelation starts the snowball of faith rolling. If people respond with the right attitude to the realization that there is someone greater than themselves, then God will send them the knowledge they need to be saved. Sometimes He does it in miraculous ways. We know that because He did so on three separate occasions in the New Testament.

In Acts 8:26–39, an Ethiopian official went to Jerusalem to worship the God of Israel, yet his knowledge of God was limited. On his way home, the official stopped his chariot to read a passage about the Messiah from the book of Isaiah. But he couldn't understand what he was reading. He was not a Jew, so the Messiah was a foreign concept to him. What did God do? He saw a heart that was right toward Him, so He miraculously sent Philip to share the gospel with this man. The Ethiopian official was saved and baptized that very day.

In Acts 10, a Roman centurion named Cornelius loved God and wanted to know Him. What did God do? He spoke to the apostle Peter in a vision and then dispatched the disciple to share the gospel with this centurion. And Cornelius became a believer.

In Acts 19:1–7, the disciples of John the Baptist were lovers of God and followers of the law, but they didn't know Jesus. What did God do? He sent Paul to share the gospel with them and lead them to a saving faith in Christ.

Whenever God sees a heart that wants to know Him, He will send His truth into that person's life. And that truth surpasses any objection people may raise against it.

Implications of Rejecting the Exclusivity of Jesus Christ

As we put in context these objections to Jesus's claim to be the only way of salvation, we need to recognize that there are also three very real implications for embracing inclusivism, the idea that all religions are equally valid.

The Personal Implication

First, there's a personal implication. If all religions are equally valid, then how do you know which god you should worship? Does it make a difference? If we pursue that line of questioning far enough, we come to a spiritual catch-22: if all roads lead to God, then we have to reject not only Christianity but also Islam and Buddhism, since they all teach that their religion is the exclusive way to God.

The Relational Implication

Second, there's a relational implication. Imagine that you're enrolled in a college biology course. On the first day of the semester, the professor announces that everyone in the class will receive a final grade of A+. No matter how well or how poorly you do, you're guaranteed the highest grade possible.

If a test question asks you to name a property of water, and you answer, "beach house," you get an A+. If you write an essay explaining that a biome is one more than a monome and one less than a triome, you get an A+. If your assigned twenty-five-page final research paper contains only one sentence, and that sentence is "Biology is a lie," you get an A+.

Knowing that an A+ is guaranteed regardless of what you do, how motivated would you be to study biology? How much effort would you put into your assignments? Would you even show up to class?

A similar dilemma confronts us if we say that all roads lead to God. If everyone is going to heaven regardless of what they do or believe, is there any reason for you to share your faith? Or to support mission efforts around the world? Or to invest your money in God's work? Is there any reason to believe your relationship with Christ is worth celebrating or talking about at all?

The Spiritual Implication

Third, there's a spiritual implication. If you believe that all people will be saved regardless of their religious faith, then you must reject the most basic teachings of Jesus Christ. At the front of that line is John 14:6, ground zero for exclusivism: "I am the way, and the truth, and the life; no one comes to the Father but through Me."

Inclusivism also renders moot Jesus's teaching on the wide and narrow gates in Matthew 7:13–14. If you embrace all religions, you're also embracing the notion that there are no gates at all but rather one gigantic superhighway leading straight to heaven.

In John 3:18, Jesus, speaking of Himself, said, "He who believes in Him is not judged; he who does not believe has been judged already, because he has not believed in the name of the only begotten Son of God." If Jesus was wrong about these key issues, how can we legitimately trust Him in anything He had to say?

How Do We Talk about the Exclusivity of Christ?

The foundational Christian doctrine that Jesus Christ is the only means of salvation sets God's people apart from every other religion. To share the good news behind this doctrine, we must go against the grain of our culture. We risk being accused of intolerance, hatred, and prejudice.

I've experienced these kinds of accusations firsthand. I am often invited to appear on cable news shows and share a biblical perspective on current events. Many times, those conversations turn to the question of the exclusivity of Christ. And even on conservative talk shows, the hosts often bristle at my assertion that there is only one way to heaven.

In this chapter, I will share some of the things I've learned about how to have respectful, informed conversations about this subject of the exclusivity of Christ. Even if we're the only person in the conversation who holds to a biblical perspective, the advantage we have is that we're speaking God's truth. We have the power of His Word behind us. We also have powerful evidence that sets our Christian faith apart from all other religions.

Present the Evidence

Of the thousands of belief systems in the world, how can we know that Christianity is the right one? There are four pieces of evidence that argue in favor of the exclusivity of the Christian faith.

First, *Jesus Christ is unique.* Most historians agree that Jesus was a historical person. And most people who acknowledge His existence believe Jesus was a good, moral person, but He certainly wasn't God. The problem with that belief is that Jesus Himself doesn't give us that option.

Unlike every other major religious leader, Jesus claimed to be God. He didn't claim to be someone who pointed the way to God, as Muhammad claimed to be, but God Himself. In John 10:30, Jesus said, "I and the Father are one." When His disciple Philip said, "Lord, show us the Father, and it is enough for us," Jesus replied, "He who has seen Me has seen the Father" (14:8–9). Before Jesus was crucified, He was brought before Caiaphas, the high priest, who asked Him, "Are You the Christ, the Son of the Blessed One?" Jesus answered, "I am" (Mark 14:61–62).

Also, unlike every other religious leader, Jesus claimed to be able to forgive sins. In Mark 2, four men brought a paralyzed man to see Jesus. "And Jesus seeing their faith said to the paralytic, 'Son, your sins are forgiven'" (v. 5). The religious leaders were furious. "Why does this man speak that way? He is blaspheming; who can forgive sins but God alone?" (v. 7).

Jesus then healed the paralyzed man to show that He was indeed God, who had the authority to forgive sins.

Alone among the major religious leaders, Jesus claimed to be able to conquer death. From the beginning of His ministry, Jesus predicted what was going to happen to Him. He said, in essence, "I'm going to go to Jerusalem, I'm going to be tried, I'm going to be executed, and on the third day I'm going to rise again from the dead."

In Matthew 16:21, "Jesus began to show His disciples that He must go to Jerusalem, and suffer many things . . . and

THE IMPORTANCE OF THE RESURRECTION

Even Jesus's enemies understood that the resurrection was at the core of His teaching. That explains why they went to Pontius Pilate, the Roman governor, after Jesus's burial (Matt. 27:62–66).

The Jewish leaders asked Pilate to secure Jesus's tomb so His disciples wouldn't steal His body and claim He had risen from the dead as He predicted. They knew if that word got out, the Christian movement would spread like wildfire. So the religious leaders did everything they could to make sure Jesus's body remained in the tomb.

Pilate shared their concern. He didn't want followers of some new religion causing a revolt in Rome. So he appointed a unit of sixteen highly trained soldiers to guard the tomb. That Sunday morning, they discovered just how fruitless their efforts had been.

Because Jesus did indeed rise from the dead, eternal life is available to everyone who trusts in Him.

be killed, and be raised up on the third day" because that was God's will for Him. Jesus's death was not accidental. It wasn't the result of bad people prematurely extinguishing His life. Jesus's death was part of God's plan to bring salvation to the world, and Jesus knew this. Furthermore, Jesus said His resurrection from the dead would be proof to everyone that He truly was the Son of God.

Finally, alone among all major religious leaders, Jesus claimed He would return to judge the world (Matt. 25:31–46). Only Jesus Christ said our eternal destiny is dependent on our acceptance or rejection of Him.

Second, *Jesus's teaching includes exclusivity.* The teaching of Jesus includes the exclusivity of the Christian faith. If you accept that Jesus is Lord, then it stands to reason you must trust everything He said. If Jesus Christ is really God, then everything He said is true.

Jesus taught there are only two eternal destinations for people. In verse 46, Jesus said the unrighteous "will go away into eternal punishment, but the righteous into eternal life." He did *not* say everyone is going to the same place when they die.

Third, *Jesus offers the only way to heaven.* That means even the sincerest followers of other religions must trust in Christ for salvation. It's no coincidence that Jesus gave His most detailed explanation of how to get to heaven not to a hardened atheist but to a devout Jew. In John 3, Jesus talked with a Jewish leader named Nicodemus, who had spent his life trying to keep the Mosaic law. If anyone should have gone to heaven on the basis of good works, it was Nicodemus. But Jesus told this respected Jewish leader that his devotion to the law was not enough. Nicodemus had to be born again. In

John 3:14–16, Jesus explained how to be born again. Whoever believes in Jesus will have eternal life. The Greek word translated as "believes" means "to trust in, to believe in, to cling to, to put your full hope and faith in."

Fourth, *Jesus offers the only genuine solution to humanity's greatest dilemma.* Almost every religion contains a kernel of truth. And one common denominator in almost all the world's religions is that humanity's basic problem is internal.

However, other religions claim that the solution for our dilemma begins with us. For example, Eastern religions such as Buddhism and Hinduism say the way we overcome our basic selfishness is through meditation, by which we empty ourselves of our desire for pleasure and status. Other religions such as Islam and Judaism say the way to solve our dilemma is by trying to earn God's favor through keeping a set of laws and regulations.

Christianity's diagnosis of the human condition is much more severe. Christianity says we're not only flawed but also spiritually "dead in [our] trespasses and sins" (Eph. 2:1). Paul said in Romans 3:23, "For all have sinned and fall short of the glory of God."

Furthermore, unlike other religions, Christianity doesn't allow selective obedience to God's law. Every other religion says do the best you can—but not Christianity. James 2:10 says, "For whoever keeps the whole law and yet stumbles in one point, he has become guilty of all." According to Romans 6:23, the penalty for falling short of God's standard is eternal death. Christianity is unique because it raises the performance requirements. Christianity doesn't say it's good enough to be good enough. Christianity says God's standard is absolute perfection. The problem is, no one can meet God's standard.

Since none of us is capable of meeting that standard, God instituted a rescue plan for us. He sent His Son, Jesus Christ, who lived a perfect life and willingly died on a cross. As Jesus hung on that cross, God poured out all the punishment we deserve for our sins on His Son. Jesus experienced hell so that we can experience heaven. God tells us, *If you will quit trying to earn My forgiveness and simply put your faith and trust in Jesus, I'll place all your sins on Him and let Him pay for them. And I'll wrap Jesus's absolute righteousness around you so that when I look at you from now on, I'll no longer see your sin; instead, I'll see the perfection of My Son.* Paul explained it this way in 2 Corinthians 5:21: "[God] made Him who knew no sin to be sin on our behalf, so that we might become the righteousness of God in Him."

God offers to forgive our every failure—not on the basis of what we do for Him but on the basis of what Christ has done for us. God doesn't require that we earn His forgiveness. In fact, He doesn't even allow us to try. In Ephesians 2:8–9, Paul said, "For by grace you have been saved through faith; and that not of yourselves, it is the gift of God; not as a result of works, so that no one may boast."

Respond to Objections

Where does that leave believers? We have an urgent message to proclaim—a matter of eternal life and death. Yet the truth we have to share is so out of step with our culture that we risk offending others with it. How do we respond to these objections to salvation? How do we help people understand that the gospel—Jesus is the only way to God and the only means of salvation—is the greatest news the world has ever received? As I've responded to these objections to the exclusivity of Jesus Christ over the years, I've found four responses that tend to help defuse tension and open the door to heartfelt conversation.

First, *"Your argument is with the Bible, not with me."* Jesus said in John 14:6, "I am the way, and the truth, and the life; no one comes to the Father but through Me." In Acts 4:12, Peter said, "There is salvation in no one else; for there is no other name under heaven that has been given among men by which we must be saved." Paul said in Romans 10:9, "If you confess with your mouth Jesus as Lord, and believe in your heart that God raised Him from the dead, you will be saved."

Jesus, Paul, and Peter were all Jews. Yet they all made it clear that no one can be saved by following Jewish rules and regulations. Only through Jesus Christ can someone be saved. As we share the gospel, it's important to point out that we're not concocting our own way to be saved. We're simply repeating what God has already said—and we do so not to hurt people but to help people.

Second, *"God wants to save as many, not as few, people as possible."* Consider the words of the three most prominent Jews in the New Testament. In 1 Timothy 2:4, Paul said, "[God] desires all men to be saved and to come to the knowledge of the truth." In 2 Peter 3:9, Peter said, "The Lord is not slow about His promise, as some count slowness, but is patient toward you, not wishing for any to perish but for all to come to repentance." In Luke 19:10, Jesus said, "For the Son of Man has come to seek and to save that which was lost."

Third, *"The fact that God has provided one way of salvation demonstrates His love, not His hatred."* Suppose you're on a plane that crash-lands. The cabin fills with smoke and the interior lights flicker out. A flight attendant stands at the front of the plane, waving her emergency flashlight, yelling, "This way out!" Would you accuse her of being intolerant because she insisted there's only one way out of the plane? If someone grabbed your hand in the darkness and said, "Follow me, I'll help you out," would you say that person was being hateful or narrow-minded? We can't force people to utilize the way of escape God has provided. But that shouldn't keep us from courageously waving the light of God's truth in this sinful, dark world.

Fourth, *"Consider the cost."* One truth that must not get lost in this discussion is that there was a person in Scripture who took this matter of exclusivity directly to God. One person, in a moment of unimaginable duress, had the nerve to question God about whether the sacrifice of Jesus Christ was truly the only means of salvation.

That person was Jesus Christ.

On the night of His arrest, as the enormity of what He was about to do settled on Him, Jesus issued an anguished plea: "My Father, if it is possible, let this cup pass from Me" (Matt. 26:39). In other words, He was saying, "Father, if there is any other way for this sinful human race to be saved and reconciled to You—one that doesn't involve My physical torture, emotional humiliation, and spiritual desolation— please let it happen."

But Jesus ended His plea with these words: "Yet not as I will, but as You will" (v. 39). Jesus came to earth for one purpose: to do His Father's will (John 5:19). So just before He became the only way to God, He needed to know He was indeed the only way to God.

Three times Jesus prayed. And then He received His Father's answer. Reassured that He was indeed the only way, Jesus gathered His friends and waited for His enemies with a calm confidence and a reenergized sense of purpose.

Jesus asked if there was another way, and God said no. The salvation of the human race would require unimaginable suffering and sacrifice for both of them. That was the cost of sin.

Therein lies the heart of exclusivity. Jesus came to earth, lived a sinless life, allowed Himself to be crucified, and rose from the dead because no one else could. He sacrificed everything for us because there was no plan B. If all roads lead to God—indeed, if *any* other road leads to God—that means the sacrifice Jesus believed was necessary really wasn't. If there is another way to God, then God lied to His Son—and this supreme act of love becomes a monstrous deception and needless bloodletting.

When we consider the cost of salvation, we understand why there is no other way.

A Final Prayer

All of us have sinned against God. The gospel is clear that we cannot save ourselves. No matter how hard we try, we cannot be good enough to earn heaven. Instead, we have to admit our sin and trust in Jesus alone to save us. When Jesus Christ died on the cross, He willingly took the punishment you and I deserve for our sins.

The biggest decision you will ever make is whether you want to pay for your own sins or whether you will accept God's payment for your sins through Jesus Christ. If you decide you want to pay for your own sins by being a good person, you will never be able to pay your sin debt. If you attempt to get into heaven based only on your good works, you will end up being condemned to an eternity in hell.

The only other option is to accept Christ's payment for your sin. You must believe that when Jesus said on the cross, "It is finished!" (John 19:30)—literally, *paid in full*—He paid your debt for you, and you must accept that payment for your sins.

If you would like to become a Christian and know for sure that one day you will be welcomed into heaven, I invite you to pray this prayer, knowing that God is listening:

Dear God,

Thank You for loving me. I realize I have failed You in so many ways. And I am truly sorry for the sin in my life. I believe that You love me so much that You sent Your Son, Jesus, to die on the cross for me and take the punishment that I deserve for my sins. And right now, I am trusting in what Jesus did for me—not in my good works—to save me from my sins. Thank You for forgiving me. Help me to spend the rest of my life serving You. In Jesus's name, amen.

8

THE CHURCH

Robert Frost wrote, "Home is the place where, when you have to go there, they have to take you in."[1] That same begrudging attitude seems to be the stance of many people toward the church. If they were to describe their relationship status with the church on social media, they would likely choose "It's complicated."

On the one hand, if you've spent any quality time in a congregation with other believers, you probably can give a testimony about how God used the church to minister to you. Maybe you recall when someone in the church took an interest in your spiritual growth or led you to faith in Jesus Christ. Perhaps a pastor or Sunday school teacher opened your eyes to a truth in Scripture you'd never seen before. Maybe church members supported you during a time of need or loss in your life. Or perhaps you can just look back week after week and thank God for the spiritual refreshment you received when you gathered to worship with other Christians.

On the other hand, if you've spent any quality time in a congregation with other believers, you've likely witnessed your share of power struggles, petty disputes, hypocrisy, and other un-Christlike behavior. At some point, you may have looked around the congregation and realized you have little in common with your fellow worshipers. But the strangeness of the bedfellows is what makes the church so uniquely potent. There must be supernatural forces at work, because there's no other explanation for why the church has thrived for two thousand years.

To properly understand this eighth core belief of Christianity, we need to know why the church started, what it brings to our lives, and what our responsibilities are as members of Christ's body.

Discovering Our Roots

Few things can trace their existence to a single moment in time. For example, the United States didn't suddenly spring into being when the last Founding Father signed his name to the Declaration of Independence. Electricity didn't announce its presence for the first time when lightning struck the key tied to Benjamin Franklin's kite. Reese's Peanut Butter Cups weren't born the instant one person accidentally dipped some peanut butter into someone else's chocolate.

One exception is the church, which can trace its existence to a single moment in time—a moment God made sure was recorded in detail. In Acts 2, Luke placed his readers in just the right place—a house in Jerusalem—at just the right moment to witness the birth of the church.

According to Luke's description, a noise that sounded like a violent wind filled the house. Tongues of fire appeared over the heads of everyone present. The Holy Spirit arrived, just as Jesus had promised in John 14. And with Him came a new institution, a new framework for continuing Christ's work in the world. The Holy Spirit's presence bound believers together in ways they had never experienced before.

The church was born. And in its founding and early years, we see the purposes for which it was created and the roles God intends it to play in the lives of His people.

Training Ground

The Holy Spirit uses the church as a conduit to pour His power into believers' lives. That means we cannot experience the Spirit's full power in our lives without being connected to a local church. After all, the church is the body of Christ, and each of us is a member of that body (1 Cor. 12:27).

Without that connection to the church, we are like severed limbs. If you were to separate my hand from the rest of my body, that hand would quickly atrophy. The same thing happens spiritually when members of the body of Christ are separated from the church. Our relationship with the Lord withers. God created the church not just to carry out His purpose in the world but also to supply spiritual power to individual believers.

As you read through Luke's account of the birth of the church, you'll discover that all 120 people present that day (Acts 1:15) suddenly gained the ability to communicate in a foreign language. This literal godsend proved to be extremely valuable, because these events took place during the Jewish festival of Pentecost, and hundreds of thousands of God-fearing Jews had made the annual journey to Jerusalem for the celebration. Many came from distant lands, where foreign languages were spoken.

Obviously, this created a communication barrier for the believers gathered that day, who had the good news of Jesus's death and resurrection to share. God solved the problem by giving individual believers a special gift—the supernatural ability to speak in languages they had never spoken before.

The Jewish celebrants who heard them were intrigued when they recognized their own languages being spoken so far from home. As they gathered to take in the spectacle, the apostle Peter seized the opportunity and delivered a powerful sermon. According to Acts 2:41, the result was that three thousand people gave their lives to Christ that day.

A closer look at God's strategy that day gives us a glimpse of His purpose for the church. He could have given the Jewish celebrants of Pentecost the miraculous ability to understand one person—Peter—and cut out over 99 percent of the middlemen. But that's not His vision for the body of Christ. Instead, God gave each believer a specific gift to use—perhaps it was one language or dialect per person.

That being the case, one believer on his or her own probably wouldn't have made much of an impression. Someone suddenly speaking Phrygian in Jerusalem may have attracted a passing glance, but probably not much more than that. Instead, it was the chorus of languages and dialects, rising together from people who had no reason to be speaking them, that attracted people's attention. It was the body of believers, working as one, that made a difference. That's how God intends the church to work.

There's another important takeaway from this account. As far as we know, everyone who received the Holy Spirit's gift that day used it—to great effect. But what if one person had resisted? What if a single believer had chosen not to use the gift, perhaps out of fear, shyness, laziness, or indifference?

Percentagewise, the impact would have been negligible. One out of 120 still puts the participation rate well over 99 percent. Yet what if the believer who chose not to exercise the gift was the one person able to speak Parthian that day? An entire group of people would have been left wondering what all the fuss was about. The Parthian visitors would have shrugged their shoulders and walked away. Every believer's gift mattered at Pentecost, just as every believer's spiritual gift matters today.

As we learned in our study of God the Holy Spirit, when we are saved, the Holy Spirit gives each of us a spiritual gift, which is both a desire and a unique power to be a part of God's ministry. The church serves as a training ground for Christians in honing our spiritual gifts, discovering how we can apply them, and maximizing their impact. The church is where we find our place in the body of Christ and learn to work with our fellow body parts.

Shelter from the Storm

My late mentor Howard Hendricks used to say, "The church is a lot like Noah's ark—if it weren't for the storm on the outside, you couldn't stand the stench on the inside."[2] Certainly, there are occasional odors that emanate from churches, as will happen whenever imperfect people gather. But there's also a relentless storm beating against us—a storm that began at just about the same time the church did.

Those early church members at Pentecost soon discovered that not everyone would respond to their message in the same way the masses did on that first day. Two powerful entities lined up against them, determined not only to prevent the spread of their message but also to punish anyone who dared to speak it.

Jewish leaders recognized the threat that Christianity posed to their own religion. Every Jewish convert to Christianity was a direct loss for Judaism. At the same time, Roman authorities feared that the growth of Christianity might lead to political upheaval. So both factions committed to stamping out the Christian faith.

History shows that Christian persecution intensified during the first century. Followers of Christ were hassled, arrested, tortured, and killed because of their faith. Alone, they were vulnerable. But together, they were a force to be reckoned with. The church provided a shelter from the storm of persecution. Believers found comfort, strength, encouragement, and motivation with other believers.

The church still provides shelter today. The consequences we face for our faith may not be as intense as those the first-century believers faced, but they are just as real. And alone, we are still vulnerable. God has given us the church to surround and protect us from the forces that war against us.

Launch Pad

The church also functioned as a launch pad for ministry and evangelism. In Acts 11:22, Luke said, "The church at

Jerusalem . . . sent Barnabas off to Antioch." The congregation selected Barnabas to serve as a missionary. According to Acts 13:1–4, while believers in the church at Antioch were fasting and praying, the Holy Spirit said to them, "Set apart for Me Barnabas and Saul for the work to which I have called them" (v. 2). In response, the church members fasted, prayed, and laid hands on Barnabas and Saul, and then they sent them on their way.

Acts 18:5 suggests Paul was able to devote himself to full-time ministry after Silas brought him a substantial financial gift from the church in Philippi. In passages such as 2 Corinthians 11:9 and Philippians 4:15–16, Paul noted the importance of the Philippians' financial support of his ministry.

Christianity spread rapidly throughout the Roman Empire—and beyond—thanks to the work of the church. And the spread continues today.

Unity in Diversity

Perhaps even more impactful than its support of missions is the church's unity in diversity. Paul said, "By one Spirit we were all baptized into one body, whether Jews or Greeks, whether slaves or free, and we were all made to drink of one Spirit" (1 Cor. 12:13). The members of the Corinthian church to whom Paul was writing were a divided bunch. They were divided over their favorite pastor. They were divided over political philosophies. They were divided over their beliefs about spiritual gifts.

Yet note how Paul addressed the divisions in the church. He didn't say, "I want you to strive for uniformity. I want you to talk alike, think alike, and believe alike in everything." Paul didn't call for that because God doesn't call for the church to be uniform. He calls for us to be unified. He calls for us to have unity in diversity.

If you're a part of a church where everyone is in the same age group, is of the same race, is from the same economic background, drives the same cars, and dresses in the same clothes, guess what? You're in a country club. God didn't call us to be a country club; He called us to be a church. And that means people of different ages, of different backgrounds, from different walks of life, coming together to worship Jesus Christ. There's a powerful witness in that coming together. The diversity of the church is one of the greatest testimonies to the might of God.

Embracing the Church's Ministries

Grocery shopping offers a window into people's preferences. There are any number of products for which generic, lower-priced alternatives are perfectly fine. We have no problem compromising on them. In contrast, there are certain items that are sacrosanct. Only one brand or flavor will suffice. On these items, we will not compromise. We will not accept any substitutes.

What falls into the latter category for you? Is it a certain brand of peanut butter? A certain variety of apple? A certain flavor of ice cream?

What about church? How willing are you to accept substitutes when it comes to worship, biblical instruction, spiritual nourishment, and sharing your faith? How likely are you to seek alternative outlets for your spiritual gift?

The Lord established the church as sacrosanct for His people. Nothing can replace it. The church is uniquely positioned to make a difference not only in the world but also in our individual lives. Every God-honoring church supplies the four ministries I just mentioned—ministries that cannot be matched anywhere else: worship, instruction, nourishment, and sharing. We cannot fully appreciate the value of the church until we understand the seismic impact these four elements have in our lives.

Worship

Worship is expressing our praise and admiration to God for who He is and for all He has done in our lives. In Psalm 34:3, the psalmist said, "O magnify the LORD with me, and let us exalt His name together." Corporate worship is Christians coming together to magnify the Lord—to make Him larger.

In that sense, worship is a matter of adjusting our focus and perspective. Consider for a moment the difference in size between a nickel and the sun. The sun is the largest object in our solar system, billions of times bigger than an ordinary nickel. Yet you can place a nickel directly in front of each eye and completely block out the sun. At close range, the nickels fill your vision, making it impossible to see anything else.

The same thing happens with our daily problems. Every day, difficulties with our jobs, our families, our health, and a variety of other things fill our vision. They block our view of God because they seem much larger than they really are. The result is unnecessary stress, anxiety, and insecurity.

We need a time every week when we shift our focus and regain perspective. Instead of looking at our up-close-and-personal problems, we need to see God for who He really is.

That's what worship does for us. In my own life, worship is a source of spiritual refreshment. Every Sunday, no matter how stressful my week has been or how many problems I have been facing, I am refreshed by being with God's people in the house of the Lord.

When we worship God, we're focusing on Him rather than our problems. We're thinking about His power, His wisdom, and His forgiveness. And the larger God becomes in our vision, the smaller our problems become. That's why worship is vital. It's a time for us to come together to focus on the greatness of God.

HOW TO GET THE MOST FROM WORSHIP

As with any other endeavor, the better you prepare for worship, the more you will take away from it. How do you prepare for worship? Get plenty of rest the night before so that you're awake, alert, and ready to hear God speak. Before you do that, though, align your thoughts. Read a chapter from God's Word before you go to bed. As you drift off to sleep, ask God to speak to you the next morning, to show you what He wants you to change in your life.

Make sure your mind is in drive rather than in neutral throughout the service. Actively voice your praise to God. Use the lyrics of the songs as your prayer to Him. Embrace the words of Jesus in John 4:23, and remind yourself that God is actively looking for people who will worship Him "in spirit and truth."

Instruction

In Ephesians 4:11–13, Paul revealed God's plan for the church: "He gave some as apostles, and some as prophets, and some as evangelists, and some as pastors and teachers, for the equipping of the saints for the work of service, to the building up of the body of Christ; until we all attain to the unity of the faith, and of the knowledge of the Son of God, to a mature man, to the measure of the stature which belongs to the fullness of Christ."

The ultimate purpose of the church is to build up believers in such a way that we resemble Jesus Christ in all His fullness—in our actions, attitudes, and affections. That's why God gives ministers to the church, to equip the saints for the work of service. A personal study of God's Word is no substitute for sitting under the preaching of God's Word. There are more commands in the New Testament to listen to the Word of God from a sound teacher than there are to study the Word for yourself.

God still works through His designated teachers in the church to instruct us. We need to be in a Bible-believing church, sitting under the preaching of those God has appointed to teach His Word. Without that, we are prone to biblical and doctrinal error that will lead us into the wrong kind of living.

Nourishment

In Acts 2:42, Luke described the early believers this way: "They were continually devoting themselves to the apostles' teaching and to fellowship." These believers were so involved in one another's lives that when one of them had a need, other Christians would sell what they had to meet that need. That's what fellowship is: involvement in the needs of other believers. That involvement can take many forms. But we need to understand there are things other believers can do for us that we can't do for ourselves.

For one thing, other believers can challenge us when we're complacent. The writer of Hebrews said, "Let us consider how to stimulate one another to love and good deeds, not forsaking our own assembling together, as is the habit of some, but encouraging one another; and all the more as you see the day drawing near" (10:24–25). The Greek word translated as "stimulate" in this verse literally means "to provoke or to irritate." When a grain of sand works its way into an oyster shell, it irritates the oyster. But something incredible results from the irritation: a pearl. A similar process happens in the church.

When we get together as believers, we ought to irritate, or stimulate, one another in a positive way to produce something good—namely, love and good deeds. One reason God puts us in the church is to initiate contact with Christians who have gifts we don't have. That way, we can become familiar with those qualities and start to exercise them in our own lives.

For example, God wants us to be giving, so He puts us in contact with believers in the church who have the gift of giving—people whose example can encourage us. He wants us to be merciful, so He puts us in contact with believers who have the gift of mercy to show us how to comfort people in distress. We need to be around other Christians who will stimulate us to be more like Christ.

Another thing our fellow believers can do is encourage

190

us when we're discouraged. Unfortunately, many Christians allow the problems of life to drive them away from the church. In doing so, they play right into the hands of our enemy. One of Satan's favorite tactics is to isolate us from other believers and then attack. If you've ever watched a documentary on the National Geographic Channel, then you know that whenever you see a scene of an animal getting separated from the herd, the next shot inevitably will be of a predator lurking nearby.

Solomon demonstrated his wisdom in Ecclesiastes 4 when he said, "Two are better than one because they have a good return for their labor. For if either of them falls, the one will lift up his companion. But woe to the one who falls when there is not another to lift him up. . . . And if one can overpower him who is alone, two can resist him. A cord of three strands is not quickly torn apart" (vv. 9–10, 12). The more believers you have bound together, the harder it is to isolate and destroy them.

In the fellowship of the church, believers can pray for us when we're going through difficult times. They can offer us encouraging words or a spiritual perspective. They can remind us we have an enemy who attempts to use our difficulties for his own purposes. We can't get any of that if we're isolated from other believers.

Our fellow believers also correct us when we stray. Sin can get a foothold in our lives if we're the only ones who are aware of it. The more isolated a person is, the more destructive that sin can become. But when we spend time in fellowship with other Christians every week, we have people who can watch out for us and lovingly confront us when they see evidence of our straying. Proverbs 27:6 says, "Faithful are the wounds of a friend." We need other believers to correct us if we begin to stray.

Sharing

The description of the church in Acts 2:47—"the Lord was adding to their number day by day those who were being saved"—shows that the early Christians weren't content just to sit and soak up the Word of God. They realized the reason they were worshiping, receiving instruction, and being nourished in the church was so that they could take the gospel outside the church to unbelievers. And that's exactly what they did.

According to Ephesians 4:12, the purpose of instruction is "equipping of the saints for the work of service." The Greek word translated as "equipping" refers to loading a ship with supplies before it sets off on a long journey.

That's God's plan for the church. Every Sunday, your pastor gives you the supplies you need to go out and do ministry the rest of the week. God is building the spiritual structure of the church. And He's not doing it beam upon beam or brick upon brick. He's doing it life upon life. And He uses the church to accomplish that work.

The last word on this topic of sharing goes to Paul, who said in Philippians 2:15, "Prove yourselves to be blameless and innocent, children of God above reproach in the midst of a crooked and perverse generation, among whom you appear as lights in the world." An individual believer appears as a single light in this dark world. And while one life can certainly point people to Christ, imagine what five hundred or five thousand lights shining together can do! That's the power of the church.

Making It Personal

For better or worse, our perspective on the church is filtered through the Western mindset of individualism. Everything is about *me*—my needs, my concerns, my preferences. How to discover my spiritual gift. How to define my purpose in life. How to feel excited about my relationship with God.

In 1 Corinthians 12:27, Paul offered some much-needed perspective: "Now you are Christ's body, and individually members of it." Our individuality exists within the larger body of Christ. That's important to remember as we address some key questions about our relationship with the church.

Do I Have to Attend?

Once upon a time, it was easy to go to church. Our culture offered little in the way of competition. Many stores were closed on Sunday mornings. Employees were rarely asked to work on Sundays. Youth sports leagues didn't schedule games on Sundays. And the only thing on Sunday morning TV was televised church services.

Today, on the other hand, competition is fierce. Any number of things, from soccer tournaments to lawn care, vie for our Sunday hours. That raises the question of how important it really is to attend church regularly.

Popular thinking is that church exists for our convenience. The congregation will still proceed through the same order of worship, hear the same sermon, and sing the same songs, whether we take part or not. So we're tempted to believe that our presence at church doesn't make much of a difference.

But that's not the case at all. Beyond our responsibility to our own spiritual well-being, which suffers every time we miss an opportunity to worship, we have a responsibility to other believers. Now, at First Baptist Dallas, where I serve as pastor, we have hundreds of thousands of people who watch our worship services online and participate in our iCampus ministry, especially those who are physically unable to come to church and people who have not yet been to a church. But we also realize that viewing a church service online is no substitute for being in God's house with God's people.

In the previous section, we talked about the things other Christians can do for us. But we must never lose sight of the fact that we, too, are those "other Christians." We have a responsibility to encourage and stimulate one another to love and good deeds. We can't do that in absentia. To be who our fellow believers need us to be, we must assemble with them, week in and week out.

When you're not present in church, there's one less voice praising God in song. One less prayer being offered at the throne of grace. One less person exercising her or his spiritual gift in the body of Christ. One less person sitting under the teaching of God's Word who will go out and transform the world. Your presence, or lack thereof, impacts other people tremendously.

Do I Have to Become a Church Member?

At First Baptist Dallas, visitors come to our church on any given Sunday. We're so happy to have those guests. But something I've been noticing is how long it takes for some guests to become members. As I've talked with other pastors around the country, they're seeing the same phenomenon: it takes longer and longer for people to become members of the local church. When I talk to guests who have been coming to our church for a while, they often say something like, "Pastor, we like the church and will continue to attend, but we're just not joiners."

There are a lot of Christians today who would put themselves in that category. The prospect of joining a church brings out the fear of commitment in a lot of believers.

But if we look past our own "*my*-opia," we can see how our willingness to join a church can benefit others. When we become a church member, we say to everyone else in the congregation, "You can count on me to be here through thick or thin. I'm not going to walk away when conflict arises; I'm going to be part of the glue that holds things together. I'm going to sacrifice my own desires for the sake of the whole. I want to take on the responsibilities of membership. This isn't just a matter of convenience for me; it's a matter of commitment and accountability." And that means a lot. Being a member of a church isn't just a responsibility or duty; it's an indescribable privilege.

How Much Do I Have to Give?

Many believers approach tithes and offerings in the same way they approach taxes: pay as much as you have to so that you don't get in trouble, but no more. And that amount, as they see it, is the tithe—10 percent of their gross income. The tithe, in effect, becomes their "dues" for attending church.

The problem with that mindset is that it overlooks two important truths. The first is that everything we own belongs to God. One problem with fixating on 10 percent is that we start to believe that the other 90 percent belongs to us, to do with as we please. The reality is that 100 percent belongs to God. Look at His words in Job 41:11: "Who has given to Me that I should repay him? Whatever is under the whole heaven is Mine." We don't own anything; we're simply managers of what God has given us.

The second truth is that, as God's money managers, we should seek the highest rate of return with God's resources. Most wealthy people rely on experts to manage their money. Those managers typically earn a percentage of the assets they invest. If a money manager does well in her investments, she receives a bigger income. So she has a strong incentive to seek a good return for the person she's investing for. The same truth applies to us as God's money managers. We should seek the highest rate of return, because we will earn a higher reward for eternity.

That was the principle behind Jesus's parable in Matthew 25:14–30. Before the master left for a long journey, he divided his assets among his three servants. The first servant was given five talents—roughly four hundred pounds of gold. He invested the talents and doubled the assets entrusted to him. The second servant was given two talents. He, too, invested them and doubled the assets entrusted to him. The third servant was given one talent. He buried it, just to be safe. He gave back to his master exactly what had been given to him—and nothing more. The master congratulated the first two servants and condemned the third. He then wisely took the third servant's talent and gave it to the first servant.

Jesus's point was this: one day we will have to give an account of what we did with the time, opportunities, and financial resources God entrusted to us. For that reason, we should always seek the highest rate of return.

That's why Jesus said in Matthew 6:19–20, "Do not store up for yourselves treasures on earth, where moth and rust destroy, and where thieves break in and steal. But store up for yourselves treasures in heaven, where neither moth nor rust destroys, and where thieves do not break in or steal." In other words, if we try to hold on to our money—to use it to buy all kinds of earthly things—one day we will be humiliated by our return. Inevitably, those things will wear out, lose value, get stolen, or be left behind. But if we invest our money in eternal things that will further God's kingdom, we will receive the highest rate of return. So the right question is not "How little can I give?" but rather "How much can I give and invest in God's kingdom?"

Do I Have to Get Involved?

Some Christians have a consumer mindset toward church—the idea that it's okay to be a mere spectator. You may think it's perfectly fine to sit in the back row, observe the service, and then slip out quickly without connecting with anyone—week after week. However, the spiritual gift you received from the Holy Spirit when you gave your life to Christ says otherwise. If you need another opinion, try Paul's words in Romans 12:6: "Since we have gifts that differ according to the grace given to us, each of us is to exercise them accordingly."

If you're not sure what your spiritual gift is, think about where your passions lie. Do you have a heart for service? A knack for explaining God's Word? A desire to show mercy? An ability to meet people's practical needs? A gift for encouraging others?

Think also about what people compliment you on—the things you've been told you're good at. Sometimes other people can spot your spiritual gift before you can.

HOW TO CHOOSE A CHURCH

The way to choose a church is to be guided by God's principles, not by personal preferences. The four elements necessary in the church—worship, instruction, nourishment, and sharing—give us a checklist of questions to consider.

For example, is the Bible the foundation of the pastor's message and all the teaching in the church? Does the music, regardless of whether it's contemporary or traditional, direct our attention toward God? Does the church offer opportunities to enhance our fellowship with other believers? Does the church care for the physical, emotional, and spiritual needs of its members? Is there an active evangelism and missions program that takes the gospel into the world? Is there something supernatural happening in the church that can be explained only by the working of the Holy Spirit?

No matter what your spiritual gift is, the only place it can be fully expressed is in the local church. That's the purpose for which it was given. That's the place where it will have the greatest impact.

Every Christian must be a part of a local body of believers, and every Christian must find a place of service in that local body of believers. No one can do everything, but everyone can do something.

The Church Is God's Idea

The final takeaway of this eighth core belief of Christianity is this: the local church is God's idea. It didn't come from some ancient hieroglyphic flowchart featuring a pastor, some deacons, and a worship leader strumming a lyre.

God created the church to fulfill His purposes in this world. He also created it as a conduit to provide the things He wants to give us. And through the church, God provides what we most need, including challenge, encouragement, and correction. The church is His instrument for pouring those things into our lives.

For us to receive those things, we need to recognize the church for what it is. Let's close with an analogy featuring everyone's favorite form of travel, flying. The airline industry is a favorite punching bag in our modern culture. It seems everyone has a horror story about lost luggage or a midflight mishap. Frequent fliers commiserate over such pet peeves as crowded seating, inconsiderate passengers, and unexpected delays.

Yet even the most aggravating of these petty annoyances is shown for what it really is when we consider the grander reality. And that grander reality is this: there exists a vehicle, weighing over 900,000 pounds, that is capable of soaring to heights of 35,000 feet (or more) at speeds of 650 miles per hour (or more). This vehicle allows people to travel almost anywhere on earth in a matter of hours. It makes what was once considered impossible commonplace.

When we fix our minds on the grander reality of air travel, that lack of leg room in coach loses a little of its ability to annoy.

The same principle applies to the church. It seems everyone has a horror story. Longtime members commiserate over their pet peeves. Yet these petty annoyances are shown for what they really are when we consider the grander reality.

And that grander reality is this: there exists an institution, called the body of Christ, that has reshaped the world in which we live. The church is the vehicle God uses to accomplish His work in our lives, in the community in which we worship, and across the globe. The Lord has designed the church in such a way that it runs at peak performance only when all its members, its various body parts, are working together.

The grander reality is that the Holy Spirit has equipped every one of us to play a key role in the church, to use our gifts to serve God and others. Through the church, God gives us the privilege of representing Christ to people who don't know Him. Through the church, He shows us our spiritual purpose and helps us experience spiritual fulfillment.

Kind of puts those petty annoyances in perspective, doesn't it?

FUTURE THINGS

S *poiler alert: this chapter gives away the ending—not just of the Bible but of the earth, the heavens, and all created beings. If you don't want to know what happens, stop reading now.*

A disclaimer like this likely wouldn't deter many people from reading further, because most of us want to know how things are going to turn out—even if we may be peeking through our fingers at some of it.

An Extraordinary Glimpse of the Future

As a planner by nature, I like to set clear goals for my personal life, family life, and ministry. There are certain things I intend to accomplish in the short term and in the long term. I like to know what's ahead of me. But the reality is, no matter how many plans I make, I don't actually know what will happen tomorrow, much less ten years from now.

As finite creatures, you and I are hopelessly limited by our vantage point in time. We can look backward at the past, but we can't see any further forward than this moment. To have any grasp of future events, we must rely on the one who is eternal.

Throughout the Bible—especially in the book of Revelation—God helps us see what we cannot see on our own. He gives us an apocalyptic yet hope-filled vision of how the final days of His original creation will play out.

Still, some people question why such information is relevant. After all, it involves biblical prophecy. And for many believers, biblical prophecy falls into the same category as advanced calculus—fascinating to a few outliers but irrelevant to everybody else.

Some people try to avoid the topic altogether by claiming biblical prophecy is too confusing. However, a closer look at Scripture suggests that's not the case; God has made His prophecies quite knowable in His Word—if not necessarily the intricate details, then certainly His general plan for closing out the age.

In Matthew 24, Jesus and His disciples had just left the temple in Jerusalem when Jesus made a stunning prediction: one day that very temple would be torn down. Understandably, His announcement piqued His disciples' curiosity. They said, "Tell us, when will these things happen, and what will be the sign of Your coming, and of the end of the age?" (v. 3). In other words, they were saying, "Lord, tell us about Bible prophecy."

Jesus's response was telling. He didn't dismiss the disciples' request or tell them the information was above their pay grade. Instead, Jesus warned them of false teachers who would try to mislead them with spurious claims. He spoke of the events of the tribulation, connecting them with the prophecies of Daniel. He offered a glimpse of the signs that will precede His second coming.

More to the point, Jesus rewarded His followers' hunger for knowledge about Bible prophecy. He *wanted* them to understand end-times events.

Some people believe that studying biblical prophecy is a fruitless endeavor since no one can know when Christ will return. After all, Jesus Himself didn't know the hour of His second coming. In Matthew 24:36, He said, "No one knows, not even the angels of heaven, nor the Son, but the Father alone." Yet even though we can't know exactly when Jesus will return, we can know the events that will lead up to His coming. And knowing what to look for is just as valuable as knowing when the events will take place.

Remember, Jesus warned about false teachers who will be intent on deceiving people in the last days. Knowing what to look for can protect us from being led astray by false teaching. That's why it's important for us to understand biblical prophecy.

Some people claim that studying biblical prophecy is unnecessary because it's irrelevant to daily life. Let's be honest: most people are not nearly as concerned with the beast in Revelation 13 as they are with the beast they work for Monday through Friday. Most people's average weeks are too jam-packed with school events and church activities for them to be concerned about some future tribulation. They wonder, *What difference does biblical prophecy make if it's not tied to daily living?* But the reality is, what's going to happen in the hereafter does matter in the here and now.

Why Should We Understand Prophecy?

In a campaign speech he delivered at the 1858 Illinois Republican State Convention, Abraham Lincoln said, "If we could first know where we are, and whither we are tending, we could then better judge what to do, and how to do it."[1] The more we know about what our future holds, the better we can prepare ourselves for it.

For all of our hesitation about delving into biblical prophecy, there are three very good reasons for making it a priority.

Prophecy Is a Major Theme of the Bible

First, prophecy is a major theme of the Bible. There are more than eighteen hundred references to the second coming of Christ in the Old Testament, plus three hundred more in the New Testament. In fact, for every one prophecy that deals with the first coming of Jesus, there are eight prophecies that deal with His second coming. Twenty-three out of the twenty-seven books in the New Testament give prominence to the theme of Christ's second coming. If biblical prophecy is that important to God, then it should be important to us as well.

Prophecy Helps Us Interpret and Apply the Bible

Second, understanding prophecy helps us interpret and apply God's Word correctly. There are entire sections—and books—of the Bible we will never understand, much less apply, if we don't understand prophecy. Prophecy is like a framework, a structure on which we hang the rest of the Bible.

Take Isaiah 65:20 as an example. The only way to understand phrases such as "the youth will die at the age of one hundred" is to realize they refer to a specific time in the future: the millennium, the thousand-year reign of Christ that will begin with His second coming. Without a proper understanding of the millennium, entire sections of Isaiah, Ezekiel, Daniel, and most other Old Testament Prophets will not make sense to us.

Likewise, without a proper understanding of future events, certain words of Jesus may be misinterpreted. In Matthew 25, the Lord talked about giving food to the hungry and drink to the thirsty, inviting strangers in, giving clothes to the naked, and visiting the sick and imprisoned. In verse 40, He said, "Truly I say to you, to the extent that you did it to one of these brothers of Mine, even the least of them, you did it to Me." The popular interpretation of this passage is that Jesus identifies so completely with the poor and needy that He gives us an opportunity to do something for Him by doing something for them. However, a closer look at the passage reveals a more specific interpretation.

Jesus was talking about the end of the tribulation, a future seven-year period on earth. When Christ returns, He will judge the people who lived through the tribulation. The basis of His judgment will be how people treated the 144,000 missionaries who were saved at the beginning of the tribulation. The way people respond to those missionaries is tantamount to how they respond to Jesus. If we don't understand biblical prophecy, we'll be tempted to take the verses of Matthew 25 out of context and apply them in a way that isn't relevant for the church today.

Prophecy Motivates Us to Live in a God-Honoring Way

Third, understanding prophecy motivates us to live in a God-honoring way. The Bible never separates prophecy from practical living. In 2 Peter 3, the apostle went to great lengths to describe the future destruction of the heavens and earth. But his purpose was something much more specific than inspiring shock and awe. In verses 11–12, Peter posed a pointed question: "Since all these things are to be destroyed in this way, what sort of people ought you to be in holy conduct and godliness, looking for and hastening the coming of the day of God?" In other words, when we consider that all these things are going to be destroyed, shouldn't we live holy, blameless lives? Therein lies the real motivation for embracing biblical prophecy.

Understanding the Timeline

With thousands of end-times prophecies to consider, the task of sorting and understanding them may seem monumental. But that task is made much easier by the fact that the Bible's prophecies align in a way that reveals a specific timeline of future events.[2] This timeline, which begins with the present age and extends to eternity, gives us an excellent starting point in understanding the ninth core belief of Christianity.

Let's take a look at some of the key events on the timeline.

The Church Age

If the church age seems familiar to you, it's because you're living in it, some two thousand years after it began. The church age is the period of time from Pentecost until the rapture (a term we will discuss in the next section), during which Gentiles are invited to participate in the blessings of the covenant God made with Abraham and his descendants in Genesis 12. In the church age, God has extended the "invitation list" to be part of God's kingdom beyond the Jews to include anyone who will accept His offer of salvation.

Throughout the Old Testament, God continually worked to draw His people into a right relationship with Him. But they resisted Him time and time again. Finally, in the New Testament, God sent His own Son, the long-promised Messiah, to accomplish the work of salvation. How did Israel respond to Jesus Christ? Most of God's people rejected Him.

But God would not allow them to thwart His plan. He wanted people to acknowledge and worship His Son, so He temporarily turned away from His people, the Israelites, and invited Gentiles (non-Jews) to share in His blessing. That invitation ushered in the church age.

So here's where we stand right now: God has temporarily set aside the people of Israel because they rejected His Son. He has given the rest of the world an opportunity to be included in the blessings of His covenant with Abraham. However, Paul made clear in Romans 11:1 that God is not through with Israel yet: "I say then, God has not rejected His people, has He? May it never be!" In verse 7, Paul referred to Israel's attitude as being "hardened." But it's a temporary hardening—one that will last until every Gentile whom God has ordained to be saved is saved. After that, Israel will be given one final chance. Until that time, we're living in the church age. And it will continue until the rapture of the church.

The Rapture of the Church

The Greek word from which we get our word *rapture* means "to snatch away." And for those who are left behind after the rapture of the church, that's probably what the event will seem like. In a single moment, all Christians, from the time of Pentecost until the moment the rapture occurs, will be caught up to meet the Lord in the air. In 1 Thessalonians 4:16–17, Paul described it this way: "For the Lord Himself will descend from heaven with a shout, with the voice of the archangel and with the trumpet of God, and the dead in Christ will rise first. Then we who are alive and remain will be caught up together with them in the clouds to meet the Lord in the air, and so we shall always be with the Lord."

There are four details in Paul's description that bear examination. The first is that, while Jesus will descend from heaven, He will not come all the way to the earth. He will descend into the sky, and that's where we will meet Him. The rapture will be a midair gathering.

The second detail is that all Christians who have died since the day of Pentecost will be raised. When Christians die, our bodies remain on earth, but our spirits go to be with the Lord. That's what Paul was talking about when he wrote, "To be absent from the body [is] to be at home with the Lord" (2 Cor. 5:8). But our separation from our bodies is only temporary. When the rapture occurs, graves will be opened and the bodies of the saved will be raised.

The third detail is that Christians who are alive when the rapture occurs will meet the Lord in the air as living beings. That means an entire generation of believers will never experience death. They will pass directly from life in this world to life in the next.

The fourth detail is that our bodies will be changed from mortal to immortal. Paul said, "This mortal must put on immortality" (1 Cor. 15:53). At the rapture, believers will receive brand-new resurrection bodies from God that are free from pain, suffering, and sickness.

Perhaps the most pertinent aspect of the rapture is its imminence. There are no prophecies that must take place before it can occur. In short, the rapture can happen at any moment.

The Judgment Seat of Christ

Contrary to what some people believe, there is not one final judgment that includes both believers and unbelievers. Unbelievers will be judged at the great white throne judgment (Rev. 20:11–15), which we will look at in a moment. But Christians will be judged at the judgment seat of Christ, which probably occurs immediately after the rapture.

Paul described this coming evaluation of believers' lives: "We also have as our ambition, whether at home or absent, to be pleasing to Him. For we must all appear before the judgment seat of Christ, so that each one may be recompensed for his deeds in the body, according to what he has done, whether good or bad" (2 Cor. 5:9–10).

Believers will one day answer to Christ for every thought, word, action, and motivation of our earthly lives. But unlike the great white throne judgment for unbelievers, the purpose of the judgment seat of Christ is not condemnation but evaluation and commendation. At the judgment seat of Christ, our lives will be evaluated by Christ—not to determine our eternal destination, since that was sealed at the moment of our salvation, but to determine our rewards in heaven.

The Tribulation

The tribulation is a seven-year period that will begin when a world leader, who is referred to in Scripture as the beast or antichrist, signs a peace treaty with Israel. The tribulation will end with the second coming of Christ.

The seven-year timeframe of the tribulation is significant in biblical prophecy. It can be traced back to a promise God made in Daniel 9. When the Israelites were in exile in Babylon, the angel Gabriel revealed to Daniel that there were 490 years left on God's stopwatch to finish His plan with Israel and usher in the millennium. The angel referred to the timeframe as seventy weeks, with each year represented as a day. Seventy weeks times seven years equals 490 years.

However, there would be a separation between the first 483 years and the final seven years—that is, between the first sixty-nine weeks and the seventieth week. The angel Gabriel explained that God would start the countdown when a decree was issued for the Israelites to rebuild Jerusalem. We know from history that this decree was issued on March 14, 445 BC.

According to Gabriel, the time from that decree until the Messiah was presented would be 483 years. On April 2, AD 32—exactly 483 years after the decree to rebuild Jerusalem—Jesus rode on a donkey through the streets of Jerusalem, and people recognized Him as the Messiah. (Matt. 21:1–10).

Gabriel further explained that the Messiah would be cut off—or crucified. After that, there would be a gap of time

PRE-, MID-, OR POSTTRIBULATION: WHEN WILL THE RAPTURE OCCUR?

Not all Christians agree on when the rapture will take place. Many Christians, like myself, hold to a *pretribulation rapture* view. We believe the rapture will occur before the tribulation, that Christians will be spared the torment of those seven years because we are safe and secure from God's wrath.

Other Christians hold to a *midtribulation rapture* view. They believe Christians will be present during the first three and a half years of the tribulation, but they will be caught up to meet the Lord in the air before the most intense suffering occurs.

Still other Christians hold to a *posttribulation rapture* view. They believe the snatching away of believers will occur at the end of the seven-year tribulation and will be almost concurrent with the second coming of Christ.

One of the strongest arguments for the pretribulation view of the rapture is the twofold purpose of the tribulation: the salvation of Israel and the condemnation of unbelievers. Neither purpose is meant for the church. The church has already been saved, so we no longer need to fear the wrath of God. Romans 8:1 says, "There is now no condemnation for those who are in Christ Jesus."

Since there is no need for the church to be on earth during the tribulation, proponents of the pretribulation view maintain that Jesus will snatch away His church to be with Him in heaven before the seven-year tribulation begins.

before the final seven years commenced. That's where we are right now. On God's stopwatch, 483 years have passed. There are seven years left for God to complete His plan for Israel, which He will do during the tribulation. His stopwatch will begin again after the rapture, as soon as the antichrist signs a peace treaty with Israel.

The tribulation will fulfill two purposes. The first is the salvation of Israel. At the beginning of the seven-year period, God will save 144,000 Jews, who will serve as His witnesses throughout the tribulation. Through the work and testimony of those witnesses, many Jews—and even some Gentiles—will be saved.

The second purpose of the tribulation is the condemnation of unbelievers living on earth. The seven-year period will be a time of God's unprecedented judgment against the world. In Revelation 6–19, John identified three series of judgments God will pour out on the earth—seal judgments, trumpet judgments, and bowl judgments—each more devastating than the last.

Armageddon and the Second Coming of Christ

According to Revelation 19, at the end of the tribulation, all the world's military forces will gather on the plain of Megiddo in Israel to wage war against the antichrist and his forces. This final world conflict is called the battle of Armageddon.

But as the armies prepare to destroy one another, suddenly their attention will be diverted upward to a sight they will never recover from—the second coming of Christ. Here's how the apostle John described it: "I saw heaven opened, and behold, a white horse, and He who sat on it is called

Faithful and True, and in righteousness He judges and wages war. . . . And the armies which are in heaven, clothed in fine linen, white and clean, were following Him on white horses. From His mouth comes a sharp sword, so that with it He may strike down the nations, and He will rule them with a rod of iron; and He treads the wine press of the fierce wrath

HOW WILL THE SECOND COMING BE DIFFERENT FROM THE RAPTURE?

Some people are understandably confused about the two returns of Christ on the prophecy timeline. There are similarities between the rapture and the second coming. However, the differences between the two events are quite pronounced.

According to believers who hold to the pretribulation view, the rapture will be a secret snatching away of the church before the tribulation. The only people who will see Jesus at the rapture are believers. At the rapture, Jesus will not return all the way to earth. Instead, believers will meet Him in the air.

In contrast, the second coming will be the visible return of Jesus Christ to earth at the end of the tribulation. His feet will touch the Mount of Olives. The entire world, believers and unbelievers alike, will see Jesus in all His majesty. Philippians 2:10-11 says the reaction to Christ's second coming will be universal: "Every knee will bow, of those who are in heaven and on earth and under the earth, and . . . every tongue will confess that Jesus Christ is Lord, to the glory of God the Father."

of God, the Almighty. And on His robe and on His thigh He has a name written: 'King of Kings, and Lord of Lords'" (Rev. 19:11, 14–16).

When Christ returns, the tribulation will come to an end. All unbelievers alive at that time will be cast into eternal punishment (Matt. 25:46), but believers who put their faith in Christ during the tribulation and survive to see His return will be ushered into the millennium.

The Millennium

The millennium is a thousand-year period that will occur after the second coming. For one thousand years, Jesus Christ will reign on earth, fulfilling God's promise to Abraham in Genesis 15. God promised Abraham that his believing descendants would one day possess a land, seed, and blessing, where the Messiah would rule on the throne of David from Jerusalem. Abraham believed Him, and so did his descendants. For centuries, the people of Israel clung to the hope of that promise.

As the days of creation wind to a close, God will demonstrate His faithfulness again. And it's vital that we understand the significance of this fulfillment. After all, if God were to renege on—or even slightly alter—His promise to Israel, what would keep Him from doing the same thing with the promise He made to us of eternal life?

Christ will initiate His thousand-year reign on earth by asserting His power over His foes, as described in Revelation 20:1–3: "Then I saw an angel coming down from heaven. . . . And he laid hold of the dragon, the serpent of old, who is the devil and Satan, and bound him for a thousand years; and he threw him into the abyss, and shut it and sealed it over him, so that he would not deceive the nations any longer, until the thousand years were completed."

With Satan bound for a thousand years, part of the curse of sin will be removed. This is the time Isaiah 65 describes, when infants will not die, when people will live to be at least one hundred years old, and when we won't have difficulty in agriculture with thorns and thistles. The millennium will see a renovation, but not a re-creation, of the earth.

Satan Released and the Final Rebellion

At the end of the millennium, Satan will be released "for a short time" (Rev. 20:3). The question is, Why would God let him go, especially when things will be going so well?

Here's what we need to understand: only believers will enter the millennium and experience the earthly reign of Christ. Those of us who were saved before the tribulation, along with the people who became believers during the tribulation and then died, will enter the millennium in our new, resurrected bodies. But people who became believers during the tribulation and survived until Christ's second coming will enter the millennium in their natural bodies. That means they will be able to marry and have children. During the thousand-year reign of Christ on earth, children will be born, grow up, and have families of their own, for generation after generation.

Keep in mind, too, that it's necessary that every person choose whether to follow Jesus. So at the end of the thousand years, God will release Satan for a short time and allow him to work his evil influence. Amazingly, some people who were born and grew up during the millennium will choose to follow Satan instead of Jesus. That is the final rebellion.

The Great White Throne Judgment

God will put an end to this rebellion once and for all at the great white throne judgment—His final judgment against all unbelievers who have ever lived. In Revelation 20:13, John described the scene this way: "And the sea gave up the dead which were in it, and death and Hades gave up the dead which were in them; and they were judged, every one of them according to their deeds." When unbelievers die, their spirits go to Hades, which is described as a place of agony (Luke 16:24). Hades is a temporary place of intense suffering for the unsaved dead as they await their final judgment.

At the great white throne judgment, all the unbelieving dead will appear before the Lord and be judged by their works. That criterion is only fair, since unbelievers say, in effect, "I don't need God's forgiveness; I'm good enough to get into heaven on my own merit." So God agrees to their terms and judges them by their works. Unfortunately, the standard by which God judges is the perfection of Jesus Christ. And by that standard, "all . . . fall short of the glory of God" (Rom. 3:23).

The result of this judgment is spelled out in Revelation 20:14–15, when "death and Hades were thrown into the lake of fire. This is the second death, the lake of fire. And if anyone's name was not found written in the book of life, he was thrown into the lake of fire." Verse 10 completes the picture: "They will be tormented day and night forever and ever."

Unbelievers will not be destroyed after they are judged; instead, they will suffer for eternity. The same Greek word that is used to describe the eternal nature of heaven is also used to describe the eternal nature of hell. The horrible truth about hell is this: when you've spent three trillion years in the agony of hell, you will not have reduced by one second the amount of time you have left. That's the fate of everyone who dies without trusting in Jesus Christ.

According to 2 Peter 3:7, 10, one final event will conclude the great white throne judgment: "By His word the present heavens and earth are being reserved for fire, kept for the day of judgment and destruction of ungodly men. . . . But the day of the Lord will come like a thief, in which the heavens will pass away with a roar and the elements will be destroyed with intense heat, and the earth and its works will be burned up."

Eternity Future

After the present heaven and earth are destroyed, we come to the events in Revelation 21. Eternity future begins. Describing his astonishing vision, the apostle John said, "Then I saw a new heaven and a new earth; for the first heaven and the first earth passed away, and there is no longer any sea. And I saw the holy city, new Jerusalem, coming down out of heaven from God, made ready as a bride adorned for her husband" (vv. 1–2).

Popular images of heaven feature believers worshiping God in an ethereal, cloudlike setting. However, as John's vision in Revelation 21 makes clear, the reality of heaven will be much more familiar to us. Our eternal dwelling place will be a new earth. Though in many ways it will seem familiar to us, it will also be very different from the earth we know. It won't be the renovated earth of the millennium. The earth on which we will spend eternity will be entirely re-created, restored to its original purpose. God will allow us to enjoy forever the world as He originally created it to be.[3]

Amazingly, our enjoyment of eternity will be enhanced by the work we do. As we saw in our study of humanity and sin, humans were created to find fulfillment and joy in work. Contrary to what many people believe, work is not a curse from God as a result of Adam and Eve's sin in the garden. Before the first couple ever took a bite of the forbidden fruit, God gave them the responsibility of work. Genesis 2:15 describes it like this: "Then the LORD God took the man and put him into the garden of Eden to cultivate it and keep it."

Although Eden was perfect, it was not self-sustaining. Humans were given the responsibility of cultivating it by tilling the soil and planting and harvesting crops. While it's true that Adam and Eve's work became much harder after the fall because of God's judgment, work has always been—and will always be—part of God's plan for us.

The only reason we recoil from the prospect of working for eternity is that our labor on earth has been burdened by the effects of sin's curse: bodies that grow tired, relationships that become strained, and an environment that is uncooperative. In the new heaven and earth, all those burdens will disappear because "there will no longer be any curse" (Rev. 22:3). In the world as we know it, work can be exhausting. In eternity, work will be exhilarating.

In eternity, our physical, mental, emotional, and spiritual well-being will be assured. Our resurrected bodies will be perfect. Cancer, heart attacks, and strokes will all be things of the past. So will blindness, deafness, and paralysis, as well as gray hair, wrinkles, and widening girths. From the top of our heads to the bottom of our feet, we'll be perfect in every way.

In eternity, God will "wipe away every tear from [our] eyes; and there will no longer be any death; there will no longer be any mourning, or crying, or pain; the first things have passed away" (Rev. 21:4). This is the forever future God has planned for those who trust in Jesus Christ.

In the Meantime

For Christians, the fact that we are currently living in the church age seems to put us in limbo, as far as the timeline of biblical prophecy is concerned. What can we do now, aside from waiting for the rapture to occur? As we discover in Scripture, there is actually much to do in the meantime. For starters, we can stay prepared, continue our work, and take comfort.

Stay Prepared

The wording Paul used in 1 Corinthians 15:52 to remind us of the imminence of the rapture is significant: "In a moment, in the twinkling of an eye, at the last trumpet; for the trumpet will sound, and the dead will be raised imperishable, and we will be changed." Whenever Roman soldiers were about to break camp and march to a new location, they would sound three trumpet blasts. The first blast meant, "Strike your tents and prepare to depart." The second blast meant, "Fall in line." The final blast meant, "March away."

In terms of prophecy, God has already sounded the first trumpet. He has reminded us that we need to strike our tents and be living as "aliens and strangers" in this world, which is about to be destroyed (1 Pet. 2:11). He has also sounded the second blast, telling us to "be of sober spirit" and "be on the alert" for His appearance (5:8). All we are waiting for is that last trumpet blast, at which time we will march away into the presence of our Commander.

Therefore, we should be "looking for the blessed hope and the appearing of the glory of our great God and Savior, Christ Jesus" (Titus 2:13). In other words, we should live with the expectation that the rapture could occur at any moment.

Continue Our Work

Until that time, we need to be salt and light in our world (Matt. 5:13–16). In our pursuit of that goal, we must remember 2 Peter 3:9: "The Lord is not slow about His promise, as some count slowness, but is patient toward you, not wishing for any to perish but for all to come to repentance."

God's patience and desire to see everyone come to repentance are all that stand between us and our eternal future. We are to spread the gospel to as many people as possible before the world is swept away by God's judgment.

The stakes could not be higher. Jesus made that point clear: "These [the unrighteous] will go away into eternal punishment, but the righteous into eternal life" (Matt. 25:46). This is not a matter merely of life and death but of eternal joy and eternal suffering.

The day is coming when that choice will no longer be available to people. But it's not here yet. The eternal fate of the unrighteous can still be avoided. Jesus stands ready to rescue anyone who calls on Him. That's the good news that must not get lost in our discussion of the end times.

In Acts 16, the Philippian jailer put the question to Paul and Silas in the simplest and most straightforward terms: "Sirs, what must I do to be saved?" (v. 30).

> What must I do to meet Jesus in the air when the rapture occurs?
>
> What must I do to be counted among the armies of Christ in the final battle between good and evil?
>
> What must I do to experience the earthly reign of Jesus Christ for a thousand years?
>
> What must I do to avoid the great white throne judgment?
>
> What must I do to be saved from the torment of the lake of fire?
>
> What must I do to enjoy forever the world as God originally created it to be? To find ultimate fulfillment in the work for which God created me? To be given a new, perfect body that will never be injured, experience disease, or grow old? To experience complete well-being? To dwell in the presence of God forever?

Paul and Silas's reply to the jailer was equally simple and straightforward: "Believe in the Lord Jesus, and you will be saved" (Acts 16:31). That's the message that should occupy our time as we await the final trumpet blast.

Take Comfort

The stark realities of biblical prophecy, especially the images of judgment and suffering in Revelation, can distract us from a very important truth: God is in control.

In Charles Dickens's *A Christmas Carol*, Ebenezer Scrooge asked the Ghost of Christmas Yet to Come, "Are these the shadows of the things that will be, or are they the shadows of things that may be, only?"[4] In other words, is the future set in stone—or can it be avoided?

The shadows of biblical prophecy fall squarely in the former category. God's will cannot be stopped, altered, or avoided. He has set the events in motion. As we saw earlier, the only reason they haven't happened yet is that God wants to give as many people as possible an opportunity to come to salvation. But this grace period will come to an end at the exact moment God has preordained and in the manner He has determined.

The world only seems to be spinning into chaos. The reality is that nothing is beyond God's control. Evil only seems to be winning the day. The reality is that the season for evil is drawing to a close. When God's plan unfolds, evildoers will never again prosper at the expense of others. Good people will never again suffer. God will take care of everything, according to His perfect timing and His perfect plan.

Jesus gave us the ideal capstone for this ninth core belief of Christianity in His words to His disciples: "These things I have spoken to you, so that in Me you may have peace. In the world you have tribulation, but take courage; I have overcome the world" (John 16:33).

10

CHRISTLIKENESS

I s there a more daunting word in the Christian vocabulary than *Christlikeness*? Can you imagine a more ambitious goal? Think about it: at a young boy's first peewee basketball practice, the coach doesn't hand him a ball and say, "Let's see some Jordanlikeness." The first time a young girl steps onto a tennis court, the instructor doesn't hand her a racket and say, "From now on, when people look at you, they should see Serena Williams." An elementary school teacher doesn't hand back a student's very first essay and say, "I expected more Twainlikeness out of you."

Yet what happens when we put our faith in Christ? We're told that Jesus is the only Son of God. He came to earth to do what we could not do for ourselves. He lived a sinless life. He never once gave in to temptation. He dedicated Himself completely to God's will. He used Scripture to drive away Satan. He demonstrated sacrificial love, the likes of which have never been seen before or since. His was the most important life in human history. Oh, and by the way, when people look at you, they should see Him.

What does that mean? As we study this tenth core belief of Christianity, we'll discover that Christlikeness is intimately tied to our relationship with God, the work of the Holy Spirit, and the way we view the world. We'll also discover that Christlikeness is not as far beyond our reach as it may seem. In fact, with God's help, it's well within our grasp.

Pursuing God's Will

What is God's will for our lives? The answer to that question is the holy grail, so to speak, of our existence. After all, once we know God's definitive will for us, we'll be able to spot every signpost and every trail marker on our walk with Christ. We'll be able to march confidently through this life, fairly certain of where we're going. Or so the thinking goes. So we pray fervently for God to reveal His will to us and wait for His grand revelation. If we're not careful, we may become frozen in place, afraid to make the wrong move, while we wait for His yellow-brick road to become apparent to us.

However, God has already revealed His will for us. It's there, for the whole world to see, in Romans 8:28–29.

Let's start with verse 28: "And we know that God causes all things to work together for good." Those thirteen words are an optimist's delight. They seem to imply that no matter how horrible something is that happens in your life, somewhere there's something good in it. And if you just look hard enough or wait long enough, you'll see the silver lining in the cloud.

What's more, these words seem to offer an insurance policy for believers. If God causes all things to work together for good, then surely that means that if we take the wrong road in life, God will turn it into an incredible journey. Or if we bungle an attempt to witness to someone or to model our faith, God will turn our clumsiness into something special. As long as there's a modicum of effort involved, whatever we do will turn out for the best.

If, in fact, that's what Paul meant by those thirteen words. But it's not.

There are some things that happen to us that are so tragic, so scarring, that to suggest good can come from them almost minimizes our suffering and our efforts to heal. That's not what Paul was promising in Romans 8:28. To get to the heart of the matter, we have to examine the verse in its entirety: "And we know that God causes all things to work together for good to those who love God, to those who are called according to His purpose."

Paul's point was that God is using everything that happens to you—the good, the bad, and the ugly—to accomplish His purpose in your life. And what is that purpose? This is going to surprise some of you. God's purpose for your life is not that you have a satisfying marriage. God's purpose for your life is not that you have a successful career or an impressive bank account. God's purpose for your life is not that you be healed from every physical disease. No. God's purpose for your life is found in verse 29: "For those whom He foreknew, He also predestined to become conformed to the image of His Son, so that He would be the firstborn among many brethren."

God loved Jesus so much that He said, in so many words, "I don't want to have just one Son. I'd love to have many children—men and women who resemble the Son I love in the things they love, the way they act, and the thoughts they have."

God's plan for you is not just to save you, to rescue your soul from hell, but to transform you, to chisel in you the perfect image of His Son. And Paul was saying that everything in your life is working together for that one purpose: to make you just like Jesus. To make you love the things Jesus loved, to do the things Jesus did, to act the way Jesus acted in every situation. Every success as well as every sadness, every triumph as well as every tragedy, is working together for that one purpose.

In my own life, I've found it's not the easy things that tend to make me more like Jesus. It's those hard things, those sad things, those things that defy our human understanding that God uses to chisel away anything un-Christlike in my life.

The process by which God conforms us to the image of His Son is known as *sanctification*, and it's a lifetime work. Your relationship with God doesn't reach its full potential the moment you're saved. God saved you to begin the sanctification process in you. Paul described it this way: "He who began a good work in you will perfect it until the day of Christ Jesus" (Phil. 1:6).

The question that arises is this: Is sanctification, our becoming like Jesus, God's responsibility or our responsibility? Some people embrace the "Let go and let God" view of the process. They say, "Just as you can't become a Christian through human effort, you can't live as a Christian through human effort. So just let go and let God take care of it." However, certain passages of Scripture seem to contradict that thinking. And they all come from the letters of Paul.

In Galatians 5:16, he said, "Walk by the Spirit, and you will not carry out the desire of the flesh." In Ephesians 4:22–24, he said, "In reference to your former manner of life, you lay aside the old self, which is being corrupted in accordance with the lusts of deceit, and that you be renewed in the spirit of your mind, and put on the new self, which in the likeness of God has been created in righteousness and holiness of the truth." And in Colossians 3:8, he said, "But now you also, put them all aside: anger, wrath, malice, slander, and abusive speech from your mouth."

Look at his message in these passages. *You* are the one who must lay aside your old nature. *You* are the one who must lay aside anger, malice, and wrath. *You* are the one who's responsible for walking in the Spirit. *You* are the one who's responsible for putting on the new self. In other words, don't wait for God to do these things for you.

Other people embrace the "If it's going to be, it's up to me" approach to sanctification. This is the pull-yourself-up-by-your-own-spiritual-bootstraps mindset that says if you just read your Bible and pray enough, you'll eventually become like Jesus Christ. But that approach won't work either. Jesus Himself said so in John 15:5: "Apart from Me you can do nothing."

That leaves only the middle ground. Sanctification, the process of becoming like Jesus, is a cooperative effort between God and us. God supplies the power; we supply the effort. Without God, we cannot. Without us, God will not.

The apostle Peter described this joint effort in 2 Peter 1:3: "His divine power has granted to us everything pertaining to life and godliness, through the true knowledge of Him who called us by His own glory and excellence." God has given us everything we need to be Christlike. And we access that power through His Holy Spirit.

Working with the Holy Spirit

In our study of God the Holy Spirit, we learned that the Holy Spirit dwells in every believer. The purpose of His indwelling is to transform us—to make us like Christ. And given the opportunity, that's exactly what He does. But He will not do it independently of us or against our will.

The Holy Spirit dwells in us, but He occupies only those areas that we surrender to His control. That act of surrendering is the key to Christlikeness. The more of our lives we choose to give over to the Holy Spirit's control, the more people will see Christ in us.

However, we must understand that while surrender is a choice, it's not a once-and-for-all decision. Every day we face dozens of situations in which we must decide whether we will surrender to the Holy Spirit or grab the reins of our lives.

For example, let's say you're browsing online when an ad for an adult website pops up. The images in the ad catch your eye, as they're intended to do. At that moment, you have a choice. Your curiosity is telling you to click on the ad and look at what you know you shouldn't. But the Spirit is saying, *Shut it down right now. Get up and walk away.* In that split second, you have a decision to make. Are you going to be controlled by your lust, or are you going to be controlled by the Holy Spirit?

Shortly after you've made that decision, you'll undoubtedly be faced with another. The process of surrendering, of working toward Christlikeness, never ends. And we won't always make the decision to surrender. The apostle Paul, the greatest missionary the world has ever known, testified to that fact. Look at his words in Romans 7:18–19: "For I know that nothing good dwells in me, that is, in my flesh; for the willing is present in me, but the doing of the good is not. For the good that I want, I do not do, but I practice the very evil that I do not want."

We can all identify with Paul's conundrum. We want to do the right thing, yet we find ourselves unable to do so. We say, "I'll never do that again," only to find ourselves doing it thirty minutes later. The only day we'll ever be completely free from our struggle with sin will be the day of our death.

The good news is that the struggle gets easier the more often we choose to be controlled by the Holy Spirit. Think of it as a habit we develop. The more often we say yes to the Spirit and no to sin, the easier it becomes the next time to say yes to the Spirit and no to sin.

What Does the Holy Spirit Do in Our Lives?

People who develop the habit of walking with the Spirit find that there are four things the Holy Spirit gives us when He has control of our lives.

Power in Times of Temptation

First, the Holy Spirit gives us power in times of temptation. He helps us understand that because we've been freed from the power of sin, we need to act accordingly.

According to 1 Peter 3:18, the Holy Spirit has made us alive in Christ. The same power of God that reached down and lifted Jesus Christ out of the grave is working in our lives right now to free us from the power of sin. To claim that power, we need to present our bodies to God every day.

That's what Paul was talking about in Romans 6:12–13: "Therefore do not let sin reign in your mortal body so that you obey its lusts, and do not go on presenting the members of your body to sin as instruments of unrighteousness; but present yourselves to God as those alive from the dead, and your members as instruments of righteousness to God." In other words, don't let sin have the final say in your life. Considering this new power you have in Christ, start acting in a way that's consistent with that truth.

Stop filling your eyes with pornographic images from movies and internet sites. Instead, start filling your eyes with the truth that comes from God's Word.

Stop using your tongue to criticize and tear down other people. Instead, start using your words to encourage and build up others.

Stop allowing your feet to take you places you know you shouldn't go. Instead, present your feet to God to take you to share the gospel with people.

Stop allowing your mind to be controlled by anger and fear. Instead, allow it to be filled with the peace that comes from the Holy Spirit.

Direction in Times of Confusion

Second, the Holy Spirit offers us direction in times of confusion. Jesus said, "My sheep hear My voice, and I know them, and they follow Me" (John 10:27). In matters of Christlikeness, there is no ambiguity. Jesus clearly communicates the direction He would have us go. Sometimes He speaks to us through His Word. Sometimes He speaks to us through prayer. Sometimes He speaks to us through the wise counsel of other believers. We need only to pay attention to His voice.

That's easier said than done in our noisy culture! So we must be proactive in our communication with the Lord. Dive deep into Scripture, and wrestle with passages you don't understand. Commit verses to memory. Continually look for ways to apply God's Word wisely in your life.

I encourage you to set aside the best part of your day, the time when you're sharpest and most alert, for prayer. "Draw near with confidence to the throne of grace" (Heb. 4:16) as you ask for God's will to be done. Tell Him your needs, your fears, your confusion, your temptations, your anger, and your sadness. And when you've exhausted your speech in prayer, listen intently to your heavenly Father, ready to take note of the things He brings to your attention.

Then take time to nurture relationships with other believers. Foster a spirit of honesty in those relationships by "speaking the truth in love" to one another (Eph. 4:15). Make the well-being of these people a priority in your life, as they do the same for you. And consider the counsel of your fellow believers, especially when they're saying things you may not want to hear.

Courage in Times of Opportunity

Third, the Holy Spirit offers us courage in times of opportunity. We see that courage illustrated in the life of the first Christian martyr. In Acts 6–7, the enemies of Christianity targeted Stephen, one of the leaders of the early church, for persecution. They made false accusations against him and then dragged him before the Sanhedrin. Knowing that the men he faced were looking for an excuse to put him to death,

Stephen launched into an epic sermon that doubled as an indictment of the Jewish religious leaders. Stephen traced God's faithfulness and Israel's unfaithfulness throughout the nation's history. He concluded by pointing out how the religious leaders themselves had broken the law and killed God's Chosen One.

The Holy Spirit gave Stephen the courage to speak boldly when the opportunity presented itself. In a frenzy, the religious leaders drove Stephen out of the city and stoned him to death. And as his life slowly ebbed away, the Holy Spirit gave Stephen the courage to forgive those who were killing him.

The passage in Acts doesn't tell us exactly how the Holy Spirit's infusion of courage into Stephen affected the people who witnessed it. But it does note that one of those witnesses was a young man named Saul—who later became the apostle Paul.

Comfort in Times of Stress

Fourth, the Holy Spirit allows us to experience comfort in times of stress. When a phone call comes in the middle of the night to inform you there's been an accident. When your doctor tells you the report is not good. When your employer tells you your services are no longer needed. When your mate tells you he or she no longer loves you. When bombshells explode in your life, you have a choice as a Christian. You can be filled with anger and fear, or you can allow the peace of God that passes all human comprehension to take control of your life.

Power in times of temptation. Direction in times of confusion. Courage in times of opportunity. Comfort in times of stress. These are just some of the benefits of being controlled by the Holy Spirit.

232

Staying Heavenly Minded in Our Earthly Surroundings

In his letter to the believers in Colossae, Paul wrote, "Therefore if you have been raised up with Christ, keep seeking the things above, where Christ is, seated at the right hand of God. Set your mind on the things above, not on the things that are on earth" (Col. 3:1–2).

God has placed believers in a difficult, though not impossible, situation. He asks us to be citizens of two worlds at the same time. Our citizenship is in heaven (Phil. 3:20), yet we are on earth to fulfill God's will.

This predicament is so unusual that it merited a special prayer by Jesus on our behalf: "I have given them Your word; and the world has hated them, because they are not of the world, even as I am not of the world. I do not ask You to take them out of the world, but to keep them from the evil one. They are not of the world, even as I am not of the world. Sanctify them in the truth; Your word is truth. As You sent Me into the world, I also have sent them into the world" (John 17:14–18).

Twice in His prayer Jesus declared that His followers are not of this world. Yet twice He also declared that God's plan is not to take Christians out of this world but to send them into the world. Therein lies the tension. How can Christians live in this world, with its responsibilities and temptations, without loving this world and being conformed to its values?

That's where Paul's instruction in Colossians 3 to be heavenly minded comes into play. To be heavenly minded means to conform our daily affections, attitudes, and actions to the image of Christ. In other words, it means loving what Jesus loves, thinking as Jesus thinks, and behaving in every situation as Jesus would behave.

Allow me to frame this discussion with an experience from my own life. Being called as pastor of my first church, First Baptist Church of Eastland, Texas, was one of the happiest and most satisfying experiences of my life. For the previous seven years, I had served as youth minister under Dr. W. A. Criswell at First Baptist Dallas. Although I really enjoyed my work in Dallas, I always knew God had a different calling for me as a pastor.

After the Eastland church voted, and we announced our decision to accept the church's call, my wife and I immediately placed our membership in our new church. We spent hours in a receiving line hugging, laughing, and crying with our new members. When we returned to our motel that evening, we were so excited about our new assignment we could barely sleep.

However, I still had responsibilities to fulfill at my former church. So the next morning we drove back to Dallas, ready to finish our work there. The following six weeks was one of the strangest periods of my life. I was living in two worlds. My work was at the church in Dallas, but my membership and future were at the church in Eastland.

I can honestly tell you that I enjoyed those last six weeks of work in Dallas more than I had the previous seven years of ministry there. The fact that I would soon be leaving removed all the stress from my job. I could do what I felt was right and say what I thought was true without any fear of the consequences. After all, I was leaving. What could they do to me?

By the same token, the fact that I would soon be leaving also gave me a fresh desire for excellence in my work as a minister. Something about being called by the Eastland church as pastor made me realize the seriousness of my vocation. So I also experienced a renewed zeal in my work that began those final weeks in Dallas and carried over to my ministry in Eastland.

Living as citizens of heaven while still residents of earth should give believers the same sense of liberation and motivation—liberation from the stress of this life, since our time here is limited, and motivation to develop the attitudes and characteristics we will carry into eternity. More to the point of the tenth core belief of Christianity, these attitudes and characteristics are the very essence of Christlikeness.

Compassion

Jesus's life was marked by compassion. The motivation for many of His miracles was His deep concern for the suffering of others. We see Jesus's compassion in Mark 1:40–41: "A leper came to Jesus, beseeching Him and falling on his knees before Him, and saying, 'If You are willing, You can make me clean.' *Moved with compassion*, Jesus stretched out His hand and touched him, and said to him, 'I am willing; be cleansed.'"

And Matthew 9:36 says this about Jesus: "Seeing the people, *He felt compassion for them*, because they were distressed and dispirited like sheep without a shepherd."

Two of Jesus's best-known parables taught the importance of compassion. In the story of the prodigal son, the father is a picture of God, patiently waiting for the return of his wayward child. Notice the father's initial reaction upon seeing his son: "While [the son] was still a long way off, his father saw him and *felt compassion for him*, and ran and embraced him and kissed him" (Luke 15:20).

In the parable of the good Samaritan, Jesus contrasted the indifference of the religious leaders toward an injured man with the compassion shown by a foreigner. The Samaritan, unlike the religious leaders of the day, was genuinely concerned with people's needs. "But a Samaritan, who was on a journey, came upon him; and when he saw him, he felt compassion, and came to him and bandaged up his wounds, pouring oil and wine on them; and he put him on his own beast, and brought him to an inn and took care of him" (10:33–34).

Consider the people in your family, among your friends, in your office, and in your church who have specific needs that you're capable of meeting. Maybe it's a need for money, clothing, or food. Or maybe it's a need for attention, an encouraging word, or a sympathetic ear. When you're heavenly minded, you will mirror the compassion demonstrated by Jesus—a compassion that made itself known through positive action.

Kindness

To act kindly toward others means to deal with them from the perspective of grace, not law. It means giving people what they need rather than what they deserve. The life of Christ illustrated the quality of kindness. Fortunately, Christ gave us not what we deserved but what we needed. Out of kindness, He gave His life for us. Paul said, "But when the kindness of God our Savior and His love for mankind appeared, He saved us, not on the basis of deeds which we have done in righteousness, but according to His mercy, by the washing of regeneration and renewing by the Holy Spirit" (Titus 3:4–5).

Paul urged believers to pass on to one another what we have been given. "Be kind to one another, tender-hearted, forgiving each other, just as God in Christ also has forgiven you" (Eph. 4:32).

Consider the opportunities you have to show kindness instead of harshness to others. If you're an employer, perhaps one of your employees made a mistake that cost your company money. Justice might say the employee should be terminated. Kindness would suggest a different course of action. If you're a parent of a teenager, suppose your child wrecks your car. Justice might say the child should be grounded for six weeks. Kindness opens the door to alternative responses.

Being like Christ doesn't mean that we never act firmly. It means that our first choice—our preferred choice—will always be to deal kindly with others.

Humility

Is there any group of people more popular or more acclaimed in Scripture than the humble? Consider just a few examples:

- "When pride comes, then comes dishonor, but with the humble is wisdom" (Prov. 11:2).
- "Whoever exalts himself shall be humbled; and whoever humbles himself shall be exalted" (Matt. 23:12).
- "Clothe yourselves with humility toward one another, for God is opposed to the proud, but gives grace to the humble" (1 Pet. 5:5).

For all its popularity and acclaim, however, humility is often misunderstood. Humility is an attitude that views our accomplishments and our failures from God's perspective. One of the quirks of human nature is that we have a difficult time maintaining a balanced view of ourselves. We usually gravitate to one of two extremes: "I'm so wonderful; how could God ever get along without me?" or "I'm just a lowly worm who can't do anything."

Scripture urges a more balanced view. "For through the grace given to me I say to everyone among you not to think more highly of himself than he ought to think; but to think so as to have sound judgment, as God has allotted to each a measure of faith" (Rom. 12:3). In practical terms, humble people exhibit four characteristics.

First, *humble people are willing to give other people credit for success.* A humble person has no trouble sharing the spotlight with others. He realizes that whatever success he enjoys in life is a collaborative effort. A wise executive will give credit to her management team for a profitable year. A wise pastor will give credit to his people for their efforts in building a growing church.

The bottom line of humility is realizing that every good thing in our lives, ultimately, is the result of God's graciousness to us. In 1 Corinthians 4:7, Paul asked some interesting questions: "What do you have that you did not receive? And if you did receive it, why do you boast as if you had not received it?" Your possessions, your children, your position, and your appearance are gifts from God. Such a realization is a powerful antidote to pride.

Second, *humble people refuse to hold on to their rights.* When we understand that every good thing in life comes from God, we will stop doggedly clinging to our rights. We will be more interested in accomplishing God's purpose than fulfilling our own agenda. Jesus Christ is the supreme example of one who was willing to give up His divine rights to accomplish God's purpose.

Third, *humble people resist the need to always be right.* After Paul's admonition in Romans 12 to have a proper perspective of ourselves, he discussed spiritual gifts. As we have seen, the Holy Spirit gives each Christian a spiritual gift—a unique passion and power to further His kingdom. Some have the gift of teaching, others have the gift of mercy, still others have the gift of giving, and so on. With those differing gifts come differing perspectives.

A couple once came to see me about their teenage son, who was running with the wrong crowd, skipping school, and habitually breaking his curfew. The father had the spiritual gift of prophecy. His solution was to throw his son out of the house. The mother had the spiritual gift of mercy. She argued for a more tempered and loving approach to their son's rebellion. Who was right? Both were. The boy needed to be firmly disciplined, but the discipline needed to be administered in a loving, restorative way.

Rather than trying to force other people to see things your way, learn to appreciate their unique spiritual gifts and perspectives. A humble person realizes that he or she does not have a corner on the truth. He or she appreciates and respects the differing gifts and perspectives of others.

Fourth, *humble people demonstrate an interest in serving others.* If we're honest, most of us would admit that we tend to value other people in proportion to how they can serve us. We select a mate we think will meet our physical and emotional needs. We hire employees who will help us fulfill our vocational goals. We choose churches that will meet our spiritual needs.

Yet Jesus had a different view of people. As far as He was concerned, people were not to be used but rather served. Referring to Himself, He said, "The Son of Man did not come to be served, but to serve" (Matt. 20:28).

Take a moment to consider what a remarkable statement that is. Jesus created us (Col. 1:16). He pursued the most ambitious and worthy goal of all: to reconcile the world to Himself. Therefore, He had every right to view us as instruments to accomplish His purpose. Yet He did not create us to meet His objectives. He came to fulfill *our* needs! As His followers, we're called to adopt that same attitude toward other people.

Gentleness

Gentleness is sometimes translated in the Bible as "meekness." Unfortunately, when we think of *meekness*, we think of the similar-sounding word *weakness*. In reality, the meaning of *gentleness* or *meekness* is power that is under control. Picture the scene from the movie *King Kong* in which the giant ape gently holds the beautiful girl in his hand. Now that's power under control!

The heavenly minded Christian is one who will not let his emotions, especially his hostile feelings, overpower him. Instead, he will respond the way Christ did on the cross. Rather than lashing out in anger at His enemies or calling down the heavenly host to judge them immediately, Jesus said, "Father, forgive them; for they do not know what they are doing" (Luke 23:34).

Patience

The Greek word translated as "patience" means "long-tempered." The word usually refers to patience with people, not circumstances. As far as the Bible is concerned, patience means more than tolerating red lights, delayed flights, or long lines at the grocery store. Patience means enduring mistreatment by others.

This idea is antithetical to what the Greeks believed. Aristotle taught that it was a virtue to strike back at insults. We hear the same attitude today in advice such as "Don't get mad; get even."

Yet the heavenly minded person not only endures mistreatment by others but actually forgives it. Paul put it this way: "Bearing with one another, and forgiving each other, whoever has a complaint against anyone; just as the Lord forgave you, so also should you" (Col. 3:13). The Greek word translated as "forgive" means "to release." That is the essence of forgiveness: letting go of people's offenses against us. Why should we do that? Because God forgave us when we did not deserve forgiveness. He forgave us unconditionally. It's our responsibility to mirror that same forgiveness toward others.

Love

Love is the quality that binds all other Christian graces together. In 1 Corinthians 13, Paul emphasized the preeminence of love: "If I speak with the tongues of men and of angels, but do not have love, I have become a noisy gong or a clanging cymbal. If I have the gift of prophecy, and know all mysteries and all knowledge; and if I have all faith, so as to remove mountains, but do not have love, I am nothing. And if I give all my possessions to feed the poor, and if I surrender my body to be burned, but do not have love, it profits me nothing. . . . But now faith, hope, love, abide these three; but the greatest of these is love" (vv. 1–3, 13).

The Greek word translated here as "love," *agape*, refers to a self-sacrificing love that is more concerned with giving than receiving. This love is best exemplified by God, who loved the world so much that He gave His Son. Paul said it is out of this basic attitude toward others that compassion, kindness, humility, gentleness, and patience flow. And it is this quality that best measures the degree of our heavenly mindedness—and our Christlikeness.

In a car engine, oil is the lubricant that makes the various moving parts run smoothly. Without it, an engine will quickly burn up. It would be very difficult to look into an engine's crankcase to see how much oil is present. Instead, the manufacturer provides a dipstick. When you pull out the dipstick, you can easily see how much oil is in the engine.

In the same way, we have a readily visible measurement of our commitment to God, and that's our love for other people. If our affections and thoughts are set "on the things above" (Col. 3:2), then our lives will be characterized by the qualities Jesus displayed: compassion, kindness, humility, gentleness, patience, and love.

Within Our Reach

In Romans 6:4, Paul said, "Therefore we have been buried with Him through baptism into death, so that as Christ was raised from the dead through the glory of the Father, so we too might walk in newness of life." Paul was saying, "You don't have to wait till you die to experience this new life. That same quality of life can be yours, because you have participated in the resurrection of Jesus Christ from the dead." You don't have to wait till you die to become like Jesus and to experience the benefits of living a Christlike life. You can experience that transformation right now.

Christlikeness is a tall order. There's no denying that. But it's never beyond our grasp—not even after we've failed spectacularly. Our Christlikeness doesn't come down to one make-or-break moment in our lives. It comes down to the dozens of decisions we make every day.

Every interaction we have, every temptation we face, every decision we make about what we will or won't do in a given situation is a new opportunity to let others see Christ in us. God has equipped us to accomplish His will. The Holy Spirit stands ready to guide us. As amazing as it sounds, we have within us the power to be like Jesus Christ.

CONCLUSION

Solid Ground

Question: What do you do after you've explored the ten core beliefs of the Christian faith?

Answer: You build.

You build with confidence, as the wise man in Jesus's parable in Matthew 7:24–27 did. You create a spiritual abode where you will be protected when the storms of life rage.

You build vertically toward God, focused on Him with all your heart, soul, mind, and strength. You explore the heights of what He can do in and through your life.

You build horizontally to include your loved ones, friends, coworkers, neighbors, acquaintances, and others. You invite them to share your foundation and build alongside you.

You use the finest materials God has made available to you—His Word, the Holy Spirit, prayer, the church, your spiritual gift, worship, and other Christian disciplines—to create something pleasing in His sight. You model your structure in part on what others have done, but you make yours unique, something that reflects what God created in you.

Construction Tips

As we wrap up our study of these ten core beliefs of Christianity, let's look at a few "construction tips"—specific ideas for building on each pillar of the Christian faith.

God's Word

From the earliest days of humanity, Satan's strategy has been to shake the foundation of this pillar. He knows if he can find some "give" in your connection to God's Word, he has an access point. Remember his question to Eve in the garden: "Did God really say . . . ?" (Gen. 3:1).

The apostle Peter recognized this vulnerability. That's why he said, "Always [be] ready to make a defense to everyone who asks you to give an account for the hope that is in you, yet with gentleness and reverence" (1 Pet. 3:15). Always be ready to explain not just *what* you believe but *why*.

The way to do that is through Bible reading and study. You need a plan to follow. For example, you might select one book of the Bible to focus on for a month. After you've chosen your plan, designate a specific time each day for Bible study. Try a new translation, such as the New Living Translation, to allow God to communicate familiar truths in a fresh way. Concentrate on smaller sections of the Bible. Remember, the goal of reading the Bible is not the completion of a task but the transformation of your life.

Look for—and follow—God's commands. Ask God to reveal timeless truths that apply to you, and develop specific steps to apply each truth. Never close your Bible without answering the question, *What am I going to do differently because of the truth I've just encountered?*

God the Father

You build on the pillar of God the Father by frontloading your prayers with praise and adoration. After all, God created us to worship Him. To help us fulfill our purpose, He's given us an infinite amount of material. It's not hard to find reasons to worship God.

The natural world has His fingerprints all over it. You can find His creative genius in everything from the design of the eyeball to the laws of physics that govern the universe. You can find His creative beauty on display in a flower garden, a wintry mountain range, and a summer sunset.

You build on the pillar of God the Father by studying His perfections, by pondering what it means that He is holy, just, loving, eternal, all-powerful, all-knowing, immanent, transcendent, sovereign, and unchanging. You learn His names so that you can use them powerfully in your conversations with Him. You find creative ways to praise God for who He is and what He's done.

God the Son

You build on the pillar of God the Son by immersing yourself in the words and actions of Jesus. You develop a working knowledge of who He is, why He came, what He accomplished, and what the implications are. You familiarize yourself with the prophecies He fulfilled. You meditate on what the Bible writers said about Him. You wrestle with His difficult teachings—what it means to love your enemies, to live as travelers in this world, and to suffer for doing good.

Satan's efforts to undermine our understanding of Jesus can be subtly effective if we're not paying attention. You build on this pillar by being able to counter people's misunderstandings about Jesus with the truth.

You acknowledge Christ as the perfect High Priest and recognize that He experienced everything you experience, from pain and rejection to temptation and weakness. The difference is that He did it without sinning. His life pleased God from start to finish, and He stands ready to help you live in a way that pleases Him as well.

God the Holy Spirit

"Let every heart prepare Him room"—so says the beloved Christmas carol "Joy to the World."[1] These words, of course, refer to the coming of Jesus, but they also express the best strategy for building on the pillar of God the Holy Spirit.

The Holy Spirit dwells within every believer, but He occupies only the areas of your life you surrender to His control. So you build on this pillar by preparing more and more room in your life for Him—one life event, one interaction, one temptation at a time.

You build on this pillar by being aware of the Spirit's presence in your life, as well as the power He offers. You learn to recognize His prompts. You acknowledge that His guidance is infinitely better than your own. And you discover and use your spiritual gift.

Angels and Demons

You build on the pillar of angels and demons by maintaining a proper perspective on these forces. Satan and his demons are formidable foes, not because they're all-powerful but because they know your weaknesses. In spiritual warfare, their weapons can include depression, anxiety, addiction, and mental illness.

You build on this pillar by recognizing that Satan's forces are helpless against God's power. They cannot capture any spiritual ground that's under the control of the Holy Spirit. You limit their destructive capabilities by not giving them room to work in your life. So you examine your motives, aims, and priorities to make sure every bit of your life remains under the control of the Holy Spirit.

You keep a proper perspective on angels and their work. You recognize angels' usefulness in accomplishing God's purposes while resisting the urge to deify them or to assign too much credit to them. You draw comfort and strength from the knowledge that angels are ever-ready to support and protect us, to stand beside us in our spiritual battles.

Humanity and Sin

You build on this pillar by exploring God's original plan for humanity—the natural world living in perfect harmony, the pleasure of work, and the fulfillment that comes from accomplishing God's purpose. Only when you understand what our Creator originally intended can you grasp the incalculable damage our sin caused.

You realize the enormity of the chasm that our sin opened and the distance it put between us and God. You acknowledge that no amount of good works is enough to gain God's favor—that we're powerless to bridge the chasm.

You build on this pillar by feeling the awful burden our sin created. The guilt of the very first sin required shedding an innocent creature's blood to cover it. In the centuries that followed, millions of innocent creatures were sacrificed to atone for our sins. You tell others about the cost of our sins and about the only sacrifice that can ultimately save us from God's punishment—the sacrifice of His own Son.

Salvation

You build on the pillar of salvation by coming to grips with the exclusivity of the Christian faith. The only one who could make the sacrifice God required for sin was Jesus Christ (John 14:6). You learn how to communicate this truth in a loving but firm way, even though you may be accused of being intolerant.

You avoid the "way of Cain," which is any attempt to approach God on your terms rather than on His terms, or any religious system that tries to earn His favor by works rather than relying on His grace.

You build on this pillar by learning to explain Christ's unique claims: to be God, to forgive sins, to conquer death, and to judge the world. You learn to express to people who accuse you of being intolerant that their objections are with the Bible, not with you; that God wants to save as many, not as few, people as possible; that God demonstrated His love, not His hatred, in providing our only means for salvation; and that we must consider the cost of salvation.

The Church

You build on this pillar by asking not what your church can do for you but what you can do for your church. You identify your spiritual gift and put it to use in your local church. You take your role in the body of Christ seriously, recognizing that others are depending on you.

You celebrate the connection to other believers the Holy Spirit makes possible. You help others in your church by making them feel welcomed and valued every week, by taking part in your church's outreach, and by working to create unity among your fellow church members.

You build on this pillar by preparing for worship and actively participating in it. You seek out people who will challenge you, encourage you, and correct you. And you do the same for others, as you stimulate one another to love and good works.

You build on this pillar by committing yourself to the church through membership. You attend regularly, recognizing that when you aren't there, there's one less voice praising God, one less prayer being offered, one less person exercising his or her spiritual gift, and one less person sitting under the teaching of God's Word who will go out and transform the world.

Future Things

You build on this pillar by acquainting yourself with the timeline of biblical prophecy, including end-times events such as the rapture, the judgment seat of Christ, the tribulation, the second coming, the millennium, and the great white throne judgment. If you can provide answers to someone who is curious about the future, you may have an opportunity to share the reasons for your hopefulness in the face of the apocalypse.

You take comfort in the knowledge that God is in control of the future and that one day evil will be punished, once and for all. You recognize the impact future events have on the present. You understand the role prophecy plays in interpreting and applying God's Word correctly. You arm yourself with the truth of God's Word so you're not susceptible to false teachers—and by sharing that truth with others.

You build on the pillar of future things by living in a way that anticipates the imminent rapture and by looking forward to the day when you will enjoy perfect physical, mental, emotional, and spiritual health in a new resurrection body. And you make the most of the pause in God's timeline to share Christ with as many people as possible.

Christlikeness

You build on this pillar by embracing Christlikeness as God's will for your life and by working with Him in the process of sanctification. You do that by surrendering control of your life to the Holy Spirit. You listen for the Spirit's voice and make choices that honor Him, recognizing that the more often you make such choices, the more natural they become for you.

You act on the courage the Holy Spirit provides in times of opportunity and by wrapping yourself in the comfort He offers in times of stress. You keep your mind on things above—by conforming your daily affections, attitudes, and actions to the image of Christ. In other words, by loving what Jesus loves, thinking like Jesus thinks, and behaving in every situation as Jesus would behave—with compassion, kindness, humility, gentleness, patience, and love.

Build Your Life on the Rock

Sand or rock. Those were the two foundation options Jesus presented in the closing words of His Sermon on the Mount: "Therefore everyone who hears these words of Mine and acts on them, may be compared to a wise man who built his house on the rock. And the rain fell, and the floods came, and the winds blew and slammed against that house; and yet it did not fall, for it had been founded on the rock. Everyone who hears these words of Mine and does not act on them, will be like a foolish man who built his house on the sand. The rain fell, and the floods came, and the winds blew and slammed against that house; and it fell—and great was its fall" (Matt. 7:24–27).

In Jesus's story, the rock represents truth, which is another word for *theology*. The sand represents everything else.

As we have seen, the truth of God is an unshakable foundation. We build on this foundation by knowing and obeying His Word, making it our top priority. When the storms of life come, a house built on shifting sand will collapse. But a house built on the firm foundation of the rock will stand.

When it comes to our lives, we choose both the foundation and what we build on that foundation. If we build our lives on the firm foundation of truth and obedience to that truth, then our lives are guaranteed to withstand any storms that come. That's why we anchor our lives on these pillars of theology.

I pray that God will richly bless you as you build on these core beliefs of Christianity. May the life you build on this bedrock foundation not only stand strong during life's storms but also glorify the one who makes your building possible.

NOTES

Chapter 1 God's Word

1. Joe Koenig, *Getting the Truth: "I Am D. B. Cooper"* (Grandville, MI: Principia Media, 2019).

2. Anna Bartlett Warner, "Jesus Loves Me," 1859, public domain.

3. This quote is widely attributed to Thomas Edison; however, the idea may have been in circulation before Edison published it. See Garson O'Toole, "Genius Is One Percent Inspiration, Ninety-Nine Percent Perspiration," Quote Investigator, December 14, 2012, https://quoteinvestigator .com/2012/12/14/genius-ratio/.

4. William Lane Craig, "'Men Moved by the Holy Spirit Spoke from God' (2 Peter 1.21): A Middle Knowledge Perspective on Biblical Inspiration," Leadership U, accessed April 5, 2022, www.leaderu.com/offices /billcraig/docs/menmoved.html?vm=r.

5. Saint Augustine, "The Confessions and Letters of St. Augustine," Christian Classics Ethereal Library, accessed April 5, 2022, www.ccel.org /ccel/schaff/npnf101.vii.1.LXXXII.html.

6. As quoted in William Barclay, "Women in Greece," in *Daily Study Bible: Letters to the Galatians and Ephesians* (London: Westminster, 1976).

7. John Wesley, *The Journal of John Wesley*, vol. 6 (London: Epworth, 1938), 1:17.

8. For more on the inerrancy of Scripture, see chapter 2, "How Can I Know the Bible Is True?" in my book *How Can I Know?: Answers to Life's 7 Most Important Questions* (Nashville: Worthy, 2012), 31–68.

9. Charles Ryrie, *What You Should Know about Inerrancy* (Chicago: Moody, 1981), 30.

10. Peter W. Stoner, "The Christ of Prophecy," in *Science Speaks* (Chicago: Moody, 1976); http://sciencespeaks.dstoner.net/Christ_of_Prophecy .html.

Chapter 2 God the Father

1. Dictionary.com, s.v. "immanent," accessed April 5, 2022, https:// www.dictionary.com/browse/immanent.

Chapter 4 God the Holy Spirit

1. For more about these Spirit-quenchers, as well as a more detailed look at the person and work of the Holy Spirit, see my book *I Want More!: Experiencing the Power of the Holy Spirit* (Dallas: Pathway to Victory, 2014).

Chapter 5 Angels and Demons

1. John Calvin, *Institutes of the Christian Religion*, vol. 1 (Grand Rapids: Eerdmans, 2009), 14:7.

2. For a more detailed study on spiritual warfare, Satan, and demons, see my book *The Divine Defense: Six Simple Strategies for Winning Your Greatest Battles* (Colorado Springs: Waterbrook, 2006).

Chapter 6 Humanity and Sin

1. Alexander Pope, "An Essay on Criticism, Part 2," *Poetry Foundation*, accessed April 5, 2022, https://www.poetryfoundation.org/articles /69379/an-essay-on-criticism.

2. John Greenleaf Whittier, "Maud Muller," as quoted in Thomas R. Lounsbury, ed., *Yale Book of American Verse* (New Haven, CT: Yale University, 1912); https://www.bartleby.com/102/76.html.

3. Pope, "Essay on Criticism."

Chapter 7 Salvation

1. For more about the exclusivity of Jesus Christ and salvation, see my book *Not All Roads Lead to Heaven: Sharing an Exclusive Jesus in an Inclusive World* (Grand Rapids: Baker Books, 2016).

2. *Webster's New World Dictionary*, second college edition, s.v. "tolerate" (New York: Simon and Schuster, 1982).

3. Benjamin Wormald, *Religious Composition by Country, 2010–2050*, Pew Research Center, April 2, 2015, https://www.pewresearch.org/religion/2015/04/02/religious-projection-table/.

Chapter 8 The Church

1. Robert Frost, "The Death of the Hired Hand," in *North of Boston* (London: David Nutt, 1914), 3–10.

2. Howard Hendricks, as quoted in Robert Jeffress, "A Winning Church," sermon, First Baptist Church of Dallas, Texas, August 14, 2011.

Chapter 9 Future Things

1. Abraham Lincoln, "House Divided Speech, June 16, 1858," in *Collected Works of Abraham Lincoln*, edited by Roy P. Basier et al., Abraham Lincoln Online, accessed April 5, 2022, http://www.abrahamlincoln online.org/lincoln/speeches/house.htm.

2. For deeper teaching about Bible prophecy, see my books *Perfect Ending: Why Your Eternal Future Matters Today* (Nashville: Hachette, 2014) and *Final Conquest: A Verse-by-Verse Study of the Book of Revelation* (Dallas: Pathway to Victory, 2020).

3. For more about what the Bible teaches about heaven, see my book *A Place Called Heaven: 10 Surprising Truths about Your Eternal Home* (Grand Rapids: Baker, 2017).

4. Charles Dickens, *A Christmas Carol* (New York: Hodder & Stoughton, 1911), 103.

Conclusion

1. Isaac Watts, "Joy to the World," 1719, public domain.

ABOUT THE AUTHOR

Dr. Robert Jeffress is senior pastor of the fifteen-thousand-member First Baptist Church, Dallas, Texas, and is a Fox News contributor. He is also an adjunct professor at Dallas Theological Seminary. He has made more than four thousand guest appearances on various radio and television programs and regularly appears on major mainstream media outlets such as Fox News Channel's *Fox and Friends*, *Hannity*, *Fox News @ Night with Shannon Bream*, and *Justice with Judge Jeanine*, as well as ABC's *Good Morning America* and HBO's *Real Time with Bill Maher*.

Dr. Jeffress hosts a daily radio program, *Pathway to Victory*, that is heard nationwide on over one thousand stations in major markets such as Dallas–Fort Worth, New York City, Chicago, Los Angeles, Houston, Washington, DC, Philadelphia, San Francisco, Portland, and Seattle.

Dr. Jeffress also hosts a daily television program, *Pathway to Victory*, that can be seen Monday through Friday on the Trinity Broadcasting Network (TBN) and every Sunday on TBN, Daystar, and the TCT Network. *Pathway to Victory* also airs seven days a week on the Hillsong Channel. His television broadcast reaches 195 countries and is on 11,295 cable and satellite systems throughout the world.

Dr. Jeffress is the author of almost thirty books, including *Perfect Ending, Not All Roads Lead to Heaven, A Place Called Heaven, Choosing the Extraordinary Life, Courageous, Invincible,* and *18 Minutes with Jesus.*

Dr. Jeffress led his congregation in the completion of a $135 million re-creation of its downtown campus. The project is the largest in modern church history and serves as a "spiritual oasis" covering six blocks of downtown Dallas.

Dr. Jeffress graduated with a DMin from Southwestern Baptist Theological Seminary, a ThM from Dallas Theological Seminary, and a BS from Baylor University. In May 2010, he was awarded a Doctor of Divinity degree from Dallas Baptist University. In June 2011, Dr. Jeffress received the Distinguished Alumnus of the Year award from Southwestern Baptist Theological Seminary.

Dr. Jeffress and his wife, Amy, have two daughters and three grandchildren.

WITH VIVID ILLUSTRATIONS, CLEAR EXPLANATIONS, AND PRACTICAL APPLICATIONS FOR BELIEVERS TODAY, this study guide will help you get the most out of the book, whether you are studying it alone, as part of a small group, or as part of a churchwide initiative.

BakerBooks
a division of Baker Publishing Group
www.BakerBooks.com

Available wherever books and ebooks are sold.

Bring Eternity to Mind
EVERY DAY

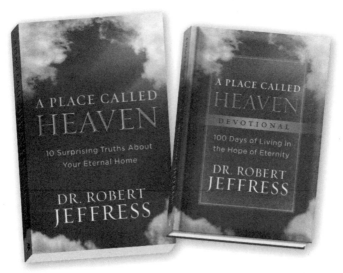

In his bestselling book *A Place Called Heaven*, Dr. Robert Jeffress opened the Scriptures to answer ten fascinating questions about heaven. Now he offers this devotional to help you think about heaven on a daily basis and put into practice the heavenly qualities of truth, honor, righteousness, purity, loveliness, character, excellence, and praise.

Colorfully illustrated and using simple concepts and language that children can understand, *A Place Called Heaven for Kids* gives children peace of mind about their lost loved ones as well as comforting, biblical pictures of their forever home.

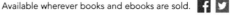

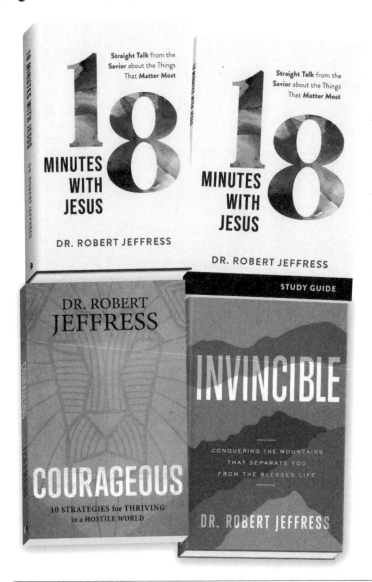
 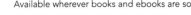

DR. ROBERT JEFFRESS
Pathway
TO Victory

To find more information about Pathway
to Victory's radio and television programs,
to check out their online store, or to
learn more about Dr. Jeffress, head to

WWW.PTV.ORG.